"*Listen Well, Lead Better* is a God-inspired book written by a God-inspired couple. Steve and Becky are passionate about real, authentic relationships with people they serve alongside, and this book will inspire and equip you to lead like Jesus."

—Evan Carlson, president, Family Life Radio

"If you lead anyone, this motivating, practical, and biblical book will show you *how* to be a listening leader who builds and blesses others all while moving the organization forward in a healthy way."

—Pam and Bill Farrel, international speakers; authors of 48 books, including the bestselling *Men Are Like Waffles, Women Are Like Spaghetti*; and co-directors, Love-Wise Ministries

"If you truly want to be a better leader, move this book to the TOP of your list. It's guaranteed not only to grow you as a leader—it will grow you as a person."

—Ron Forseth, founding executive editor, ChurchLeaders.com

"I've known Steve and Becky Harling for years, and I've watched them walk through good times and very challenging times in leadership. They are leaders of integrity who are intentional to listen well so that they might lead more effectively."

—Dr. Jim Garlow, lifelong pastor; CEO, Well Versed

"If you want to grow, if you want to lead effectively, this book will provide you with the necessary secret. Steve and Becky lead readers through thought-provoking stories and self-reflective questions to become the listening leaders that others want to follow."

—Greg and Julie Gorman, founders, Married for a Purpose

"Steve and Becky Harling are the real deal, and these pages deliver an authentic invitation into leadership that is communal, not just institutional."

—Matt Heard, lead pastor, Northland Church; founder, THRIVE

"The Harlings have written an immensely practical guidebook for caring, listening, and self-aware leadership. Get equipped to reach your destination with an intact and healthy team."

—Daniel Henderson, founder/president, Strategic Renewal

"This book is chock-full of practical advice on how to listen better, such as great questions to ask, which is so important to listening well."

—Bruce Johnson, president, SIM USA

"This book provides wisdom, insight, and practical tools to shape vision and influence people in a Jesus-hearted way. You'll get valuable help for every rung of the leadership ladder."

—Carol Kent, executive director, Speak Up
Ministries; author, *Speak Up with Confidence*

"*Listen Well, Lead Better* is packed with ear-opening insights that will help you increase self-awareness and engage those you lead and love at a deeper level of soul. Lean in and listen to what these communication experts have to say!"

—Tim Lucas, founder and lead pastor, Liquid
Church; author, *Liquid Church: 6 Powerful
Currents to Saturate Your City for Christ*

"Steve and Becky provide leaders with the tools they need to establish trust, increase discernment, and communicate effectively. By applying the techniques Steve and Becky share, leaders who read this book will certainly broaden their spheres of influence."

—Ellie Nieves, president and CEO,
Leadership Strategies for Women

"Steve and Becky's honesty and transparency in sharing successes and failures is valuable, and entertaining! Their practical tips and questions make it easy to implement healthy practices immediately."

—Kim and Bob Westfall, founders, Uncaged/Westfall Gold

"With refreshing transparency, the Harlings provide a practical tool that revives what appears to be a lost art in leadership—good listening. If you are serious about leading, this book is an excellent place to start."

—Rick Whitted, speaker; workplace consultant;
and author, *Outgrow Your Space at Work*

LISTEN WELL, LEAD BETTER

LISTEN WELL, LEAD BETTER

Becoming the Leader People Want to Follow

STEVE HARLING, BECKY HARLING

BETHANYHOUSE
a division of Baker Publishing Group
Minneapolis, Minnesota

© 2020 by Rebecca Harling and Stephen Harling

Published by Bethany House Publishers
11400 Hampshire Avenue South
Bloomington, Minnesota 55438
www.bethanyhouse.com

Bethany House Publishers is a division of
Baker Publishing Group, Grand Rapids, Michigan

Printed in the United States of America

ISBN 978-0-7642-3398-2
Library of Congress Control Number: 2019949903

Cover design by LOOK Design Studio

Authors represented by The Blythe Daniels Agency

20 21 22 23 24 25 26   7 6 5 4 3 2 1

This book is dedicated to our son,

Josiah Harling (JJ).

JJ, what a joy for us to watch you grow
up to become an incredible leader
who empowers others by listening to their hearts.
We're so very proud of you.

Mom and Dad

Contents

1

The Missing Ingredient
to Greater Influence

Tune your ears to wisdom, and concentrate on
understanding.

—Proverbs 2:2 NLT

> **Key:** The secret sauce to your
> leadership is your ability to listen.

M any leaders are missing one of the most essential in-
gredients to greater influence. They might be great vi-
sionaries, super implementers, and profound orators,

but if they don't listen well, they're leading beneath their potential. I (Steve) know this all too well.

I became a pastor right out of college, leading a little turn-of-the-century church in a farming community. The church building wasn't impressive, but we had good people.

I loved that church and was loved by the people. I was eager to lead it well. I went to every pastor's conference I could afford. I learned the guiding principles of church growth. I started to get noticed, and doors were opened over the ensuing years to lead other larger churches. Eventually, I was invited to become the lead pastor of a megachurch with scores of staff and hundreds of ministries.

Within weeks of my new appointment, I'd articulated a big vision featuring a $30 million expansion plan to accommodate seven thousand worshipers every weekend. Brimming with confidence and passionate about my vision, I didn't have time to waste. I figured that everyone would fall in line behind my leadership like rookies at basic training. Didn't happen.

While the early adopters were with me, the rest of the leadership was left in the dust . . . including the chairman of the elder board. He and I lived on different planets. Our ideas about worship, teaching, and leadership were light-years apart. I was a visionary flying at forty thousand feet. I considered him an analytical bean counter lost in the weeds. I didn't understand him. I didn't understand the people who supported him. I'm sad to say that I didn't care to understand them. I was called by God. As far as I was concerned, they needed to line up behind the vision of God's anointed (me). They didn't.

Our private feud went public. It was Outwit. Outlast. Outplay. I became more entrenched in my views. They became more entrenched in theirs. Two years into our titanic battle for control of the church, the board of elders had had enough. Both of us were put out to pasture.

Looking back, I wish I'd handled things differently. If I'd listened, I could have defused the conflict. If I'd listened, I could have established trust with the congregation. If I'd listened, I could have built ownership around the vision. Sometimes our greatest mistakes become our greatest learnings.

I am blessed today to run Reach Beyond, a global missions agency with staff and partners scattered around the world. When I first stepped in as the CEO, Becky and I made the strategic decision that we would lead by listening. In our first year, we visited every part of the world where our people serve. We asked lots of questions and did a lot of listening. Those meetings were invaluable. They helped us get branded and bonded to the organization, and they provided us with the relational insight that we needed to chart a new course.

All those trips and meetings also made something else very clear to us: We can't possibly anticipate every situation and detail. To lead to our fullest potential, we've had to fine-tune our listening skills and develop some new habits.

Like Steve, I (Becky) have had some hard-earned leadership lessons through the years. At one church, I felt confident about my vision for our small-groups ministry. We had assembled an implementation team, but my ideas were getting pushback from one particular member of the team. I would walk away from meetings thinking, *I want to quit! I'm not doing a good job. She doesn't see my vision. I need to communicate it more clearly!*

In my mind, I wasn't being compelling enough, so I would gather more information and prepare my arguments for the next meeting. The problem with that? I had forgotten a well-accepted observation: 80 percent of good communication involves listening.

Finally, I sought some advice from a friend on the team, someone who was an executive in a large company. She listened attentively as I expressed my frustration until I finally asked, "How am I coming across?" I'll never forget her response. She first shared her view that my so-called adversary was an external processor. What I saw as combative was merely a person trying to figure out her feelings by processing out loud. Finally, my friend said, "When she processes, and you get tense, you talk more instead of listening and drawing her out. As a result, you come off a bit insecure and defensive." Ouch!

My friend was exactly right. I have to admit that I was insecure in my leadership in those days. Whenever I felt insecure, I shut down and withdrew, became defensive, or came on too strong to prove my point. God began to whisper in my ear that He had plans to use me as a leader, but that in order for Him to use me I needed to learn to listen. I wanted others to follow, but I didn't understand that in order for them to feel motivated to follow, they needed to feel heard.

About fifteen years ago I got serious about my listening skills and began intentionally working on them. I became certified through the John Maxwell Team as a leadership coach. I learned how important it is to listen attentively, to ask great questions, and to offer others value by being fully present. As my listening skills grew, so did my influence.

The expanse of your leadership platform is directly linked to how well you listen. No one wants to follow someone who won't listen to others. The truth is, many leaders have lost their credibility because they haven't put any effort into their listening skills. Once credibility is lost, it's mighty hard to regain. The key to building loyal, empowered, and engaged teams is to listen attentively.

Ask Yourself

What about you? You're a leader. Or you want to be a leader. That's what compelled you to pick up this book. Leadership is influence. If you don't listen, you give up your influence. Take a few moments to ask yourself a few questions: What kind of listener are you? Would your colleagues describe you as a good listener? Does your team feel heard and valued by you? Why is it so important anyway? Aren't leaders supposed to tell others what to do?

Yes, leaders are supposed to give direction, but if they don't first listen, and the thoughts and concerns of others are ignored, disaster will often follow. We need only to look back in history to see that this is true.

In 1912 the *Titanic* sank. Many historians now believe that the root cause of the tragedy was that leadership didn't listen. According to an article in *Entrepreneur* magazine, investigations revealed that key engineers "tried to discuss the limited safety capacity with senior-level management. However, their efforts . . . fell on deaf ears."[1] The result of leaders not listening was catastrophic!

According to a Gallup poll, only one-third of Americans are fully engaged in their work.[2] When Gallup explored this further, the leading cause for disengagement in the workplace is lack of effective communication. Leaders aren't listening. On the other hand, managers who held regular team meetings and listened to their teams had a much more vested team. Gallup also found that engagement was highest among employees who had some form (face-to-face, phone, or digital) of daily communication with their managers. Managers who used a combination of face-to-face, phone, and electronic communication are the most successful in engaging employees. Those who respond to calls and messages within twenty-four hours make their staff members feel heard and valued.

We're guessing you're thinking, *I'm so overwhelmed I can't return all those emails within twenty-four hours!* Or, *I can't have that many face-to-face meetings with everyone on my team. Impossible!* We get it. To be truthful, we both fail at this from time to time. We try, but because of delayed flights, lack of sleep, volume of emails, or plenty of other excuses, we often blow it! So we're ready to offer you grace if you'll offer grace to us. But the point is, people need to feel heard and valued if they're going to stay engaged and productive. It's up to us as leaders to figure out how best to deliver that: texts, phone calls, emails, or face-to-face. Figuring that out demonstrates that *you're willing to lead by listening.*

What if you asked your team, "How would you like me to communicate with you? Is text, email, or video conferencing best for you to feel heard and connected with me?" Can you imagine how the tone would change when you ask them how they would like to feel heard by you? Game changer!

The research is clear. If you don't *listen*—and listen well—you'll probably sabotage your leadership and you might wind up sinking your nonprofit, church, or company. If you are a person of faith, there's even more at stake here than just your leadership.

What's Faith Got to Do with It?

Listening is important to God. The Old Testament book of Proverbs alone has at least twenty-two verses that either extol the value of listening or teach some concept of listening. In the New Testament the call to listen well is often repeated.

- "Consider carefully how you listen" (Luke 8:18).
- "Everyone should be quick to listen, slow to speak and slow to become angry" (James 1:19).

Jesus modeled listening leadership with the woman at the well (John 4:1–26), the blind man by Jericho (Mark 10:51), and the religious leader Nicodemus (John 3:1–21), to name just a few. It was important to Jesus to hear the hearts of those He served and draw out their thoughts and concerns. He didn't just preach great sermons and do awesome miracles. Jesus listened, asked great questions, and offered His full presence. He didn't lord it over people or treat them as somehow lesser than himself. Instead, He listened to their stories, invited them to join Him, and served them with a humble ear. He invites those of us who lead others to follow His example of listening. He said, "For those who are not listening, even what they think they understand will be taken away from them" (Luke 8:18). Pretty strong words.

Unfortunately, while many of us claim to follow Jesus, we are failing miserably at listening. We would rather assert ourselves in order to climb the corporate ladder and prove our significance than answer the questions that are written on the faces and in the hearts of those we lead. Theologian Dietrich Bonhoeffer said it so well: "The first service one owes to others in the community involves listening to them. Just as our love for God begins with listening to God's Word, the beginning of love for other Christians is learning to listen to them. God's love for us is shown by the fact that God not only gives us God's Word but also lends us God's ear."[3] I think many of us have forgotten that this is our first and primary responsibility as leaders.

Recently, while traveling in Australia, I (Steve) was craving a spiritual conversation with a stranger. It happened in a taxi cruising along the shoreline of downtown Sydney. The taxi driver had grown up in Somalia and migrated with his family to Australia. We had a great chat about his faith and what he thought about God and Jesus. As we neared the airport, I offered to pray for him and then asked him one last question: "What advice do you have for me as I relate to Muslims around the world?" His answer didn't surprise me, but it did disappoint me. He replied, "Christians don't listen. They don't even try to understand us. They just tell us what to think." Ouch, that hurt! I believe that Omar was overgeneralizing, but I'm grieved that he has that perception of Jesus' followers. I wonder how many others share his view.

Wouldn't it be extraordinary if the followers of Jesus were widely known and respected for being people who asked good questions and genuinely concentrated on understanding others? Wouldn't it be helpful if we were known for listening rather than telling . . . understanding rather than demanding to be understood?

So where are we going with all this? We want to help you become a more successful leader who has a more loyal team. We want to see your influence grow and your organization thrive. We want your team to feel heard and valued so they feel inspired to reach their fullest potential. All of that can only happen as you intentionally work on your listening skills. *But,* you might be wondering, *does listening mean I'm going to agree with everyone on everything? Or that I'm going to be able to get everyone to agree with me?* No. Before we go any further, let's just clarify what we're not saying and then we'll get to what we are promising.

What We're Not Saying

- **Listening means agreeing.** Not true. As a leader, you will seek to listen to make the other person feel heard and understood. That does not necessarily mean you'll acquiesce to them or that they will agree with you. Each person has the right to their own opinions.

- **Listening means you'll wait to make decisions until everyone is on the same page.** Not true. As leaders we believe in consensus building. However, it is unrealistic that everyone will agree. There are some decisions that have to be made even when others are not in agreement.

- **Listening means everyone will love you and you won't get criticized.** Not true. Jesus was a phenomenal listener, but not everyone loved Him. He certainly had His share of critics. The same will be true for you. More people will like you if you listen, but don't count on everyone liking you.

Our Promise to You

We can promise you that if you practice the skills outlined in this book, you will become more influential and trustworthy as a leader. Your organization will experience more success as people feel valued and heard. You'll create a culture of collaboration and cooperation. Team members will be more engaged and feel more empowered. Does that sound good to you? If you're an emerging leader and want to grow your leadership skills, the principles in this book will help you. You'll have to decide to commit to working on these skills and we must warn you, they don't come naturally. But the results will be worth the effort.

Throughout the rest of this book we're going to examine how to listen so that you can:

- Become more self-aware and less self-absorbed
- Know and understand your people
- Give the gifts of trust and empowerment
- Invite others to help shape the vision
- Discern unspoken values
- Look for truth in criticism
- Engage conflict constructively
- Listen to collect stories and build brand evangelists
- Create sacred space for personal reflection and listening to God

Our promise is that as you learn to "tune your ear to wisdom, and concentrate on understanding" (Proverbs 2:2 NLT), your leadership and your team will be transformed.

While many of the examples we share throughout the book are about high-level leaders, the lessons are for anyone who has influence or wants to increase their impact. This could include young professionals who are looking to grow their leadership skills, coaches, teachers, leaders in neighborhood associations, or leaders of the PTA, for example. The bottom line is that if you want to increase your influence, you must first learn to listen.

If you learn to make people feel heard and valued, people will want to follow you. Team loyalty will soar. How can we claim this? Because we've seen it happen. Not just in our ministry but in the many companies and ministries we've worked with. When you prioritize your listening ear and tune in to what others need, you'll find that the respect others have for you will grow and the breadth of your influence will expand. It may not always come quickly or in ways you expect, but it will come. So what can you expect from this book?

What You Can Expect

Each chapter will include teaching points, stories, and keys to enhance your listening skills as a leader. In addition, at the end of each chapter, you'll notice two categories of questions: "Questions to Ask Your Team" and "Questions for Self-Leadership." We encourage you not to skip these sections. As you practice asking your team questions and give them permission to be honest, trust in your leadership will grow. As you reflect and answer the self-leadership questions, you'll become more aware of both your strengths and weaknesses regarding your listening. These questions are designed to help you analyze where you'd like to grow as a leader both in terms of listening to your team and understanding yourself.

Here's your first set of questions:

QUESTIONS TO ASK YOUR TEAM

Preface these questions by explaining to your team that you want to work on your listening skills, so you'd like to ask them a few questions. Invite them to be honest and assure them that there is safety in their honesty.

1. What's one area of my listening that you'd like to see change?

2. On a scale of 1–10, with 1 being almost never to 10 being often, how often do I interrupt you or other team members?

3. Do you feel like you have adequate time with me to process your thoughts and concerns?

4. Do you feel safe to share new ideas, or do you feel as though new ideas are met with pushback?

5. When I'm in a meeting, does it seem as though I am fully present or distracted?

6. Describe for me a time when you felt I was being defensive. How did that make you feel?

═══ QUESTIONS FOR SELF-LEADERSHIP ═══

1. How would you describe yourself as a leader? Are you more of a consensus builder or an autocrat?

2. Do you consider yourself more of an extrovert or an introvert? How does that impact the way you listen?

3. Is it difficult for you to be patient when someone is talking? Do you find yourself hurrying them up by trying to complete their sentences?

4. What has to change in the culture of your team or organization for people to feel safe enough to share their opinions?

5. What do you like best about your personal leadership style?

As we move ahead, you'll want to take inventory of your growth. You'll need to be intentional for your listening skills to develop. You'll also need to shift your focus from all the clutter in your mind to the thoughts and feelings of others. For many leaders, that can be a challenge, but it's a skill well worth the effort. As we said earlier in this chapter, Jesus was highly focused on the needs of others. Any sense of self-preservation or advancement was set aside for the sake of others. We're convinced that God wants to see your impact grow and your leadership flourish. Ready to begin? Read on.

2

Become Self-Aware, Not Self-Obsessed

But who can discern their own errors?

—Psalm 19:12

> **Key:** Great leaders pay attention to
> how they're coming across.

While attending a conference for leaders and speakers, we heard this startling statement: "The higher a person rises in leadership, the less self-aware they often become." Wow! Scary thought! We can't verify if that's true because the statement wasn't backed up with statistics. However, the authors of *Strengths Based Leadership*, Tom Rath and Barry Conchie, write, "All too often, leaders are blind to the obvious when it comes to something of critical importance to them—their own personality. Many political and business leaders have self-concepts that are miles away from reality."[1]

As we thought about that statement, our minds traveled back to the beginning of our ministry life together.

As I (Steve) mentioned earlier, our first church was in a rural farming community. We were located next to a chicken farm. Of course, there was no air-conditioning in our ancient building. On hot summer days, we opened the fragile stained-glass windows to get some air into the sanctuary. Within minutes, the odor of fresh chicken poop invaded every nook and cranny of the building. We didn't have a lot of sophisticated people in our church. The pews were too hard and the smell was too bad. Our church was for humble folk. We had a bunch of farmers, truck drivers, day laborers, and widows. Good people. Simple people.

Imagine my surprise when one Thursday afternoon I got a phone call from a polished leader/preacher who had hit the big time in our part of the country. "Is this the little Brethren church near Lambertville?" he asked.

"Ah, yes . . . well, one of them," I replied.

He introduced himself. At first I wondered if it was a prank call. I couldn't believe that I was talking one-on-one to such a famous guy. "Well, as you know," he said, "I'll be speaking at Madison Square Garden this Saturday night. I'd love to come and preach in your church Sunday morning. I learned to play the organ there when I was a kid." Of course, I immediately agreed to give him my pulpit.

As soon as I hung up the phone, I called the Christian radio station in the nearby town. They agreed to promote our big Sunday morning event. Then we made up flyers and distributed them to all the farmhouses in the community. Saturday morning, we set up dozens of chairs in an overflow area. This was a big deal. Our little country church was on the map. We were hosting one of the most famous preachers on our side of the continent.

Sunday morning came. The pews filled up an hour ahead of time. The deacons hustled to set up projection equipment in the fellowship hall. At 10:45 I was getting nervous. Where was our speaker? The evangelist still hadn't shown up at 11:05. Our eighty-six-year-old organist had just finished a second round of her dreary prelude. We needed to get this thing going. I got up and welcomed everybody. We started singing hymns. Still no speaker. I took the offering. Still no speaker. I started thinking of a sermon that I could pull out of my back pocket. We sang some more. Still no speaker. Then, just in time for the sermon, the rear doors of the church flung open and the famous speaker and his wife came strutting down the center aisle. Every eye was on them, smiles all the way. I was relieved . . . and spent.

Turns out, the speaker went to the wrong church! That was his first embarrassment of the morning. It should have been a hint of what was to come. After a brief introduction, he did his thing. Everything went well.

27

After the service, we invited him and his wife to our vintage parsonage for dinner. We also invited a couple of our friends to join us. The speaker showed up in our dirt driveway flaunting a brand-new yellow Cadillac convertible. "Like my new wheels?" he said. I was impressed.

As Becky went into the kitchen to quickly prepare dinner, my friend and I chatted in the living room with our famous guest. The conversation went something like this:

"Well, as you know, I'll be debating _____ (the world's most famous atheist at the time) in Houston this Tuesday. Then, as you know, I'll be speaking in the Dolphins' stadium in Miami on Thursday." He went on and on. It was "As you know" this and "As you know" that. I could tell that my friend was starting to get agitated. He was a new believer in Jesus, and the way that the famous preacher was coming across didn't seem to line up with the humility of the Jesus that my friend was just now coming to know.

When dinner was ready, we assembled around our old mahogany dining table. I was at one end of the table, the evangelist at the other. My friend was seated next to the guest speaker.

I had hoped that with the start of dinner, the man of God would stop talking about himself and start asking questions of my friend. He didn't. It was more of the same. Nonstop. Finally, my friend came unglued. He couldn't take it anymore.

He suddenly interrupted the pompous preacher. "You keep saying 'As you know' this and 'As you know' that.

Until today, I didn't even know your name!" Wow! The guest speaker was stunned. His wife blurted out, "How dare you speak to my husband that way!" My friend brazenly replied, "Ever since we got here, you haven't stopped talking about yourself. You never once asked me anything. You don't listen. You just talk." I wanted to crawl under the table and hide. Becky quickly escaped to the kitchen to refill coffee cups. The well-known leader caught his breath. "Well, let's go outside and settle this." I was terrified that a fistfight was going to take place.

As it turned out, the punches never flew. My friend spoke calmly and transparently. The famous leader apologized. They came back in. We had dessert. They left. I took an aspirin and went to bed.

I can't throw the leader under the bus because I've been guilty of nearly the same. Recently we were out to dinner with some friends when I realized that I was monopolizing the conversation. I was so excited about what our organization was doing around the world that I was talking nonstop and never coming up for air. Our poor friends weren't getting a word in edgewise. Becky finally kicked me under the table. It was a not-so-subtle signal to shut up! With all my blabbering, I was completely unaware of how I was coming across. It's great to have a wife who's not afraid to deliver a timely and well-deserved kick to the shins!

The writer of Proverbs was dead-on when he wrote, "Fools deceive themselves" (Proverbs 14:8 NLT). The psalmist asked, "Who can discern their own errors?" (Psalm 19:12).

Sometimes it's just plain difficult to see the truth about how we're coming across. But if we don't figure it out, the potential of our leadership will suffer. We're guessing you don't want to be known as a leader who's full of himself (or herself).

The answer is to grow in self-awareness.

What Is Self-Awareness?

Let's admit it: If we're honest, most of us are pretty self-absorbed. Think about it. Who's the first person you look at when a group photo is taken? Yourself, right? You want to be sure you look okay before that photo goes up on Facebook or Instagram. Let's be clear, self-awareness is entirely different from self-absorption. Here's how we define self-awareness:

> **Self-awareness is a keen awareness of your strengths and weaknesses and how you come across to others.**

Here are some of the characteristics of leaders who lack self-awareness as compared to leaders who are self-aware:

Leaders who lack self-awareness

- Are clueless about how they are being perceived by others
- Talk about themselves and their accomplishments rather than drawing others out

30

- Portray body language that more often speaks of intimidation rather than invitation
- Like to talk about their accomplishments and try to make themselves look better than they actually are

On the other hand, leaders who are self-aware

- Recognize when they've taken over the conversation and are quick to apologize
- Ask questions that draw others out rather than talking about themselves
- Willingly ask for and accept feedback in an effort to grow
- Are quick to affirm the strengths and accomplishments of others

Your credibility as a leader is at stake. If you perceive yourself as a great communicator who listens well, but your staff experiences you as a leader who interrupts, gives quick solutions, and appears distracted, you'll lose respect. In the end, your leadership will suffer and you'll never live up to your potential. This is why it's important to face the truth about how you're coming across. Only by facing the truth will you be able to continue to grow as a leader.

Jesus made a profoundly insightful observation when He said, "Then you will know the truth, and the truth will set you free" (John 8:32). Truth and freedom always go hand in hand. In other words, you have to face the truth if you want to change. Only as you face the truth about your leadership skills are you able to let go of practices that are hindering your influence and effectiveness. The question is, how? How do we as leaders face our faults and become more self-aware without becoming morbidly introspective?

Self-Awareness Begins with Humility

Humility is not often talked about in leadership circles. It is seen by some as weak; yet nothing could be further from the truth. Humility is actually having the courage to have an honest assessment of yourself. It's having the strength not to flaunt all of your brilliance to the world and the restraint not to share your opinion about every little thing. When you're humble, you don't crave or cling to power and prestige; instead, you seek to value others and advance them (Philippians 2:3–4). When you're humble, you let others praise you and you let go of the need to be viewed as the expert.

Interestingly enough, often those who lack humility struggle the most with insecurity. I know, right?! Shocking! You would think it was the opposite. Author and leadership expert Brené Brown writes, "When I look at narcissism through the vulnerability lens, **I see the shame-based fear of being ordinary.** I see the fear of never feeling extraordinary enough to be noticed, to be lovable, to belong, or to cultivate a sense of purpose."[2] When you lead out of fear or insecurity, you try to fill up your own cup of self-worth, and your listening and leadership suffer. Instead of focusing on what your team members are saying, you put them in the uncomfortable position of having to prop up your ego.

We all have fears and insecurities. Every leader out there has been afraid. When you feel vulnerable, your natural instinct is self-protection. And in the words of Brené Brown, you put on armor. You might become the expert, trying to convince everyone that you absolutely know best. Or you might become cynical and roll your eyes. You might make passive-aggressive statements, in jest of course, but your sarcasm shows you feel insecure. You might hustle to insert yourself into every issue of the organization—invited or not—to prove your worth.

If you want to listen well and lead better, it's time to take off your armor. While it may protect your ego, it labels you defensive and ultimately makes you look foolish. Take the time to figure out how you respond when you feel insecure. Don't tell yourself the lie that you never feel insecure, because the truth is that every leader out there has moments of self-doubt and vulnerability. The key is to know your triggers and the armor you put on when you go into defensive mode. If you don't, you'll end up embarrassing yourself when your armor is exposed before everyone.

As you contemplate Jesus' statement about truth being what sets you free, think about some of the truths He has spoken over you:

- You have worth as God's child—you don't have to prove yourself the expert.

- You have a fan in Jesus—you don't need continual applause from others.
- You have a sovereign God who is in control—you don't need to control everything
- You have God's kingdom to build—you don't need to build your own kingdom
- You have grace in Jesus—you can admit your mistakes without trying to save face.

Jesus had a profound sense of self-awareness. He knew who He was and why He had come. He was secure in those truths and had grounded confidence in why He had been sent. As a result, He didn't need protective armor. God wants to see our confidence grounded in the truth He speaks about us so that we can find the courage to face our weaknesses authentically. Once we've faced our shortcomings, we can ask the Spirit of God to help us change so that we become more effective listening leaders.

The question is, how? How do we become more self-aware? Just as the writer of Proverbs said in the quote at the beginning of this chapter, it's so hard for us to recognize and admit our own faults. We need a little help from our friends and colleagues to become more self-aware.

Dare to Ask for Feedback

One of the best ways to grow in self-awareness is to dare to ask others for feedback. We've developed a list of great

questions to ask your friends and colleagues. Before we get to
those questions, you need to have a self-management meeting
where you establish a few rules before you invite feedback.
During your self-management meeting, remind yourself that
your value is not at stake here; you're simply trying to grow
and strengthen your leadership abilities by becoming a better
listener. Then commit to these three rules:

> **Rule #1**—Let go of defensiveness. Simply listen and say
> thank you for the feedback.
>
> **Rule #2**—Take time to pray and reflect on the feedback
> you've received.
>
> **Rule #3**—Commit to personal growth.

After you've committed to those three rules, it's time to
take action and ask for feedback. Be very careful here not
to use intimidation but to ask with humility. Sit down with
a team member after the meeting and explain that you are
working on your listening skills and that you would like their
feedback on how you came across during the meeting. Now,
they must understand that you want them to be brutally honest, or this won't work. If you're known for being willing to
receive only positive feedback, you're going to need to work
hard on rebuilding trust before you can expect others to be
honest with you. But asking for honest feedback is a step
in the right direction. Below you will find ten questions to
ask your team. We recommend asking these questions with
reference to a specific meeting. If your co-workers are honest,

you should receive some good feedback on where you might need to do some work.

Personal Reflection

After you've asked your team the questions listed below, ask yourself the questions listed under "Questions for Self-Leadership." Spend some quiet moments reflecting on both sets of answers and then write out some goals for yourself.

We're not suggesting morbid introspection, but a little reality check is in order for most leaders. Daring to ask will quickly clarify your own personal growth points. After you've received feedback, take some time to be alone and reflect. Ask God for specific ways you can change. Take a moment and echo the prayer of the psalmist David: "Search me, O God, and know my heart; test me and know my anxious thoughts. Point out anything in me that offends you, and lead me along the path of everlasting life" (Psalm 139:23–24 NLT).

═══════ QUESTIONS TO ASK YOUR TEAM ═══════

1. Did I talk too much, or did I listen well?
2. On a scale of 1–10, with 1 being not often at all and 10 being a constant problem, how often did I interrupt others?
3. How was my tone when the conversation became tense?

4. What did you see in my body language? Was it defensive or relaxed?

5. Did I seem fully present or distracted?

6. Did I allow others the time to fully express themselves, or did I cut them off?

7. Did I demonstrate that I was aware of what others in the room were feeling, or was I oblivious to their feelings?

8. At any point in the meeting did you sense I became defensive?

9. Did I allow others to have the spotlight, or did I dive in with my own story?

10. When I disagreed, did I do so in an honoring way, or did I demean the other person?

QUESTIONS FOR SELF-LEADERSHIP

1. What contributes to most of your on-the-job stress?

2. When you feel hurried, how do others in the office experience you?

3. How often do you check your phone, social media, or text messages during meetings?

4. When have you felt like you were at your best?

5. How do you want others to experience you today?

6. What is working well in your life? To what do you attribute that?

7. What is not working well in your life? What do you need to do to promote change?

8. When you feel overwhelmed, what are your coping mechanisms?

9. When self-doubt arises, how do you deal with those messages?

10. When you feel tired or burned out at work, what best revives you?

3

Know Your People

Put your heart into caring.

—Proverbs 27:23 NLT

> **Key:** Listening well builds connections and makes people feel known and valued.

Steve and I (Becky) travel a lot, and we have some quirky flying preferences. Steve has a thing for window seats. He can lean against the side wall, put in his earbuds, and zonk out. I, on the other hand, am claustrophobic and love the aisle. So quite often, Steve is at the window, I'm on the aisle, and there's a person in between us. Steve winks at me from the window seat, and we basically stay quiet about the fact that we're married so the person in the middle doesn't feel uncomfortable. It's really kind of flirty and stealthy!

On one flight, a well-dressed lady took her seat between us. Steve propped up against the window, gave me a wink, put in his earbuds, and closed his eyes. I pulled out my book to read, but the lady between us put her hand on my arm and started in with, "You know, I get really nervous when I fly!" Without pausing for me to respond, she continued to say that she was in real estate and was on her way to close the deal on another condo. The beauty of the place she was buying was in the community around it. There would be dinners and activities for all the guests. Her husband didn't enjoy the dinners, but she loved them because then she didn't have to cook. She told me about her current husband and then why she and her ex got a divorce. Then she told me all about her siblings and her mother and her mother's funeral. When the flight attendant came by offering drinks, I thought I might finally be able to crack open my book. Nope! Not. A. Chance. Taking a quick swallow of her wine, she continued on to the topic of food and drinks. I learned about which foods she liked and the wine she preferred. By the time the flight landed, I could even tell you her weight—and no, I didn't ask—she just told me. I honestly couldn't believe how vulnerable she was with a total stranger.

We exited the plane and my new friend waved good-bye, saying, "It was so great to meet you. Such great conversation!"

Steve started laughing and said, "Wow, Beck! What was that all about? She never even came up for air!" Even though he had noise-cancelling earbuds in, Steve had overheard the constant chatter. We had a good chuckle together. Later that evening, I got to thinking about how desperate people are to feel known and heard.

People Want to Feel Known

Embedded deep in our DNA as humans is the desire to feel connected and known. Kyle Benson, a relationship coach, said it this way: "*Attunement* is the desire and willingness for someone to travel into your inner world to explore who you are and who you are becoming. . . . This connection cultivates trust."[1]

We want people to trust us as leaders, and attunement builds trust. This is what the wise writer of Proverbs was getting at when he wrote, "Know the state of your flocks, and put your heart into caring for your herds" (Proverbs 27:23 NLT). He wasn't talking about literal flocks of sheep. Throughout the Old Testament, shepherding was a metaphor for leadership. The bottom line is that leadership comes with the responsibility of caring for and affirming our people and helping them to rise to their greatest potential.

Feeling Connected

Feeling connected is critical for the human soul. People want to feel a sense of belonging. Creating an atmosphere of connection while maintaining professional boundaries isn't always easy, but the payoff is huge. Part of feeling bonded is feeling heard and understood during the good times in life as well as the more difficult times. It's knowing that you have strong relationships that you can count on when life is going well and when there is a crisis.

In *How to Listen So People Will Talk*, I (Becky) told the story of how our daughter Bethany worked for a financial company who understood how important it was for team members to feel connected. "When she was first hired, her boss challenged her to conduct fifteen-minute interviews with every employee who worked for the company. She was instructed to visit with each employee and ask them to tell her their story. Bethany's first several weeks were focused very little on finances and much more on getting to know her co-workers."[2] As we've thought about the concept of every new employee conducting fifteen-minute interviews to get to know their co-workers, we think it's a great idea. Imagine how the culture of your organization might change if you put that policy in place.

Know When There's a Crisis

In every team member's life, there will be challenging seasons, and how you respond as a leader is crucial. Often, leaders make the mistake of believing that team members should leave all their personal baggage home. That's a mistake. As Solomon wrote, "Put your heart into caring" (Proverbs 27:23 NLT). In other words, don't just listen with your head; listen with your heart. People bring their whole selves to the workplace, and as leaders we need to be prepared to respond accordingly. So you might be wondering, *How do I respond when a team member is struggling or having a crisis?* Great question! Here are a few thoughts:

The best way to lead when a staff member is having a crisis is to offer understanding by **listening, empathizing,** and then **empowering.**

Listen

Cultivate the practice of compassion and create the space to be available. Care personally. Ask thoughtful but sensitive questions that can help you gain insight into the crisis that your team member is experiencing. Focus your listening on **understanding** the problem, **not fixing** the challenge. The more you seek to understand, the more your team member will feel valued. Often leaders forget that relationships, not power, move you toward success.

In her book *Radical Candor*, author Kim Scott describes walking into her office one morning and having three long conversations: the first with a colleague who had just discovered he might need a kidney transplant, the second with a team member whose child was in the ICU, and the third with an employee whose child had just received high scores on a standardized math exam. Kim felt "worn out—frustrated that I couldn't get any 'real' work done." Later, while talking with her leadership coach, she vented, "Is my job to build a great company . . . or am I really just some sort of emotional baby-sitter?"

Her coach wisely replied, "This is not baby-sitting. . . . It's called management and it is your *job*!"[3]

When you're tempted to do something "more important" than listening, remember, your leadership will rise or fall on your relationships. Learn to walk slowly through the building, taking note of your co-workers. Let go of rushing so that you can tune in to how others are feeling.

In *How to Listen So People Will Talk*, I (Becky) wrote about how important it is to use inviting signals if you want others to talk to you. Some of the signals I mentioned were:

- **Leaning.** When you lean toward someone while they're speaking, they feel like you're interested.

- **Smiling.** I remember in one ministry we served we had a very cranky receptionist working the front desk. Whenever I stopped by the office to visit Steve and saw her frown, I became nervous. I often turned around and left. Smiling is so important; I think it's a key requisite for anyone working the front desk in any office.

- **Eye Contact.** People don't trust those who don't have good eye contact. Eye contact is a huge part of building trust and connection. Learn to look people in the eye whenever you are listening.

- **Nodding.** When a person is sharing something that is important to them, nodding sends the message that you understand and want them to continue.

- **Avoiding a Shocked Face.** If you allow shock to register on your face, often the person sharing will shut down and stop talking. Instead, practice keeping your face calm.

- **A Bounce in Your Step.** A bounce sends the signal that you're happy to be there. Recently, I (Becky) was speaking at an event in Upstate New York. A group of women who had read *How to Listen So People Will Talk* approached me and, laughing, one told me, "We were watching to see if you had a bounce in your step as you went up to the platform, and we were glad to see that you practice what you preach!" It was a reminder to me that audiences of all kinds are out there watching and looking at your signals. Don't send signals that you hate work or that you're not happy to be there. If you send negative signals, you'll not likely get the promotion you're desiring.[4]

Empathize

According to the Center for Creative Leadership, empathy in leadership is more important now than ever. "The nature of leadership is shifting, placing a greater emphasis on building and maintaining relationships. Leaders today need to be more person-focused and be able to work with those not just in the next cubicle, but also with those in other buildings, or other countries."[5] Today's leader needs to be able to collaborate, traverse cultural boundaries, and motivate others toward shared values and vision between social groups with different histories, perspectives, values, and cultures. How can you accomplish all that without empathy?

Empathy is "the ability to identify with another person's feelings and circumstances"[6] It helps people feel they're not alone. Understanding is key to a person feeling connected and valued. This is the idea behind the apostle Paul's statement, "Rejoice with those who rejoice; mourn with those who mourn" (Romans 12:15). Empathy helps people feel that their feelings make sense and that someone is with them in their difficulty. It sends the clear message, "Me too! I have felt that same way." Empathy is what prompted Tarana Burke to start the "Me Too" movement. The movement blanketed social media and addressed the pervasive problem of sexual harassment and assault in the workplace.

The great news is that it is possible to build your empathy muscles. Giving time and attention to people actually fosters empathy. Here are a few tips to get you started:

TIPS TO EFFECTIVELY EMPATHIZE

- Silence your inner fixer when someone shares a problem.
- Seek to understand by asking questions.
- Validate feelings ("I understand why you feel overwhelmed.")
- Ask, "How can I help?"

In addition, leadership coaches can help you strengthen your empathy skills. The bottom line is that empathy in the workplace matters a great deal. People who feel heard and understood work harder and experience more happiness than those who don't feel valued.

Empower

You cannot fix another person's problem, but you can empower them to rise above their circumstances. How? One of the best ways to empower your team members is to show them that you trust their ability to cope and find solutions. Sometimes people just need to know that someone believes in them and their ability to overcome.

You might be able to empower by offering an employee benefit to cover counseling or coaching costs to strengthen coping techniques. One nonprofit organization that we have worked with offers to cover half the price of counseling if an employee has a crisis. Investing in the emotional health and resiliency of the staff is an important value to them. Or you might offer support by adjusting work hours. On occasion team members might need the option of working remotely as they journey through a crisis.

When our daughter Bethany and son-in-law Chris were in the process of adopting their middle son, Chris needed some extended time off from work to take care of details. He had to work remotely for at least five weeks through the process. The company Chris was working for at the time offered understanding and support. As a result, Chris felt empowered and was able to focus on family demands while still being able to keep up with work demands.

An empathic and empowering boss goes a long way when there is a crisis. Beyond knowing when there's a crisis, take the time to know each team member's strengths.

Know Their Strengths

I (Becky) had been invited by a local nonprofit to give a devotional to a ministry team. I arrived early enough to scope out the meeting space. I quickly asked my host if we could form a circle with the chairs. She assured me that was fine. After I gave my devotional from Philippians 1 on the importance of affirming those we value, I instructed team members that one by one they were going to affirm the person seated to their right. As each team member listened and received affirmation, the atmosphere in the room changed dramatically. Tension gradually ebbed and tears of appreciation began to flow. Some team members had never felt so valued. It was a good reminder to me that people desperately need to be affirmed!

People are profoundly impacted when you know and understand them enough to affirm their strengths.

In "The State of the American Workplace," Gallup reported that when employees become aware of their strengths, their productivity increases 7.8 percent. Teams that focus on strengths every day have 12.5 percent greater productivity. In addition, individuals who use their strengths every day are six times more likely to be engaged on the job and less likely to leave their company.[7]

Every one of us has been created with unique talents; God designed and hardwired our brains with certain strengths. These areas of strength mean that a person can perform certain tasks with ease and excellence. Conversely, each person has areas of weakness. When trying to perform in those areas, a person becomes frustrated and tense. A person performing in areas of weakness becomes drained at work rather than energized. As a result, balls are dropped and over-all performance levels decrease. If leaders become students of their team members, listening attentively and seeking to discover strengths, everyone in the company benefits. Job satisfaction rises and team members thrive. It's a win-win for everyone.

This is a biblical principle. The apostle Paul wrote at length in his letter to the Corinthian church about spiritual gifts and natural talents. Every ability a person is endowed with is given by God and carries with it responsibility. Whether a natural talent or "spiritual gift," these abilities are given by God for the common good (1 Corinthians 12:7). The wise leader takes time not only to recognize these gifts but also to call out those gifts in their team members.

We came across this quote in *Forbes* magazine: "The simple truth is that if we stop trying to 'fix' our employees and rather focus on their strengths and their passions, we can create a fervent army of brand evangelists who, when empowered, could take our brand and our products to a whole new level."[8] The key is focusing on your team members' strengths, but in order to focus on those strengths, you need to know their strengths.

In one of the churches we served, I (Steve) hired an administrative assistant who had recently retired from a significant role with the Veterans Administration. As it turned out, Bruce was overqualified to be my assistant. But I really loved Bruce! He was intensely likable and had an uncanny ability to make people feel at ease. His compassion quotient was off the charts.

One day Bruce informed me that he'd been diagnosed with cancer. Fortunately, the doctors thought that it had been caught early, but there was still plenty of uncertainty. We prayed together. Over the next several months, he was in and out of the office as he navigated his way through surgery and radiation treatments. Thankfully, his treatments were successful, and Bruce was eventually deemed cancer-free. Shortly after receiving the good news, Bruce bounded into my office asking if he could start a support group for cancer survivors. It sounded like a good idea, but Bruce had no training or experience with pastoral care. I gave him a hesitant okay.

Within a few weeks, Bruce had gathered a significant flock of cancer survivors for his support group and they began to meet every other week. I attended a meeting or two . . . and was amazed! With no formal training in pastoral care or theology of ministry, Bruce was hitting it out of the park as a shepherd of souls. I was incredibly impressed!

Within a few months, Bruce's cancer support group drew the attention of a noted cancer treatment center. They invited him to tell the story of his cancer-support ministry on camera. They flew him first-class to Chicago, picked him up in a limo, and housed him in a five-star hotel while they shot video of him telling his story. I couldn't have been more proud of Bruce! We had discovered Bruce's true gifts. Needless to say, I fired him as my administrative assistant and made him the Director of Pastoral Care.

We recognize that it takes time and deliberate intentionality to really know your team members. Here are a few practical suggestions to help you get started.

Practical Steps to Knowing Your Team

Maintain an open-door policy. While you can't keep an open door for everyone, you can keep an open door for those who are your direct reports. An open door sends the message, "I value you and your opinion." Team members who feel they have access to their leader are more likely to work harder to accomplish the shared goals of the organization. A wise leader gives his/her team members access and a listening ear.

On the other hand, leaders who close their doors and shut their blinds distance themselves from their team members, abdicate some of their leadership, and create opportunities for dissension. We've seen this far too often. If the leader is disengaged and unavailable, others take it upon themselves to step in. The wise leader keeps his door open whenever possible and listens attentively to the concerns of his team.

We understand that some leaders are extroverts and some are introverts. For the introverted leader, a continual open-door policy could be exhausting. If, however, there are several hours each day that you have an open-door policy, people will adjust to your expectations.

Practice walk-about management. Rather than sitting in your office all day, walk around to different offices and cubicles. It will be good for your metabolism and your member care. As you stop and visit each office, notice the photos that people have on display. Ask about the people in the photos. Make it a point to listen to what's happening in their lives.

Have virtual coffee with team members. Many companies are striving to save costs and encouraging team members to work remotely. With tools like Zoom, Microsoft Teams, or FaceTime, it's easier than ever to have virtual coffee with someone in order to get to know them better—you're drinking coffee while meeting online! This works well in our organization because team members are spread out all over the world. Having virtual coffee creates a warmer, more connected feel with very little effort.

Listen for an opportunity to affirm. Tune your ear to listen for the strengths of people. Rather than entering a meeting with the sole focus of implementing your plan to solve a particular problem, shift your focus to affirming.

According to Jim Kouzes and Barry Posner, authors of *The Leadership Challenge*, "The most genuine way to demonstrate that you care and are concerned about other people as human beings is to spend time with them. This shouldn't be yet another business meeting; instead, plan on unstructured time."[9] It is often during these unstructured times that the leader can listen specifically for strengths and then affirm.

In one of the ministries where we served, Steve orchestrated a paintball outing for the staff. He armed all the administrative assistants with paintball guns; the pastoral staff had to make it across the field on crutches, weaving between bales of hay, dodging paintballs. Amidst laughter and lightheartedness, Steve was able to get to know his staff more fully, and as a result he was able to affirm them more intelligently.

Create a growth culture. One temptation that leaders face is putting a team member in a box. What do we mean? This is when the leader assumes that a certain team member will always behave in a given manner. This is a huge mistake. Team members need permission to grow. When you as the leader recognize and affirm strengths in your people, you give the person permission to grow.

I (Steve) heard one of my vice presidents give a report that was outstanding. Later, in the privacy of my office, I affirmed him in his ability to present and create content—I challenged him to write training material for Reach Beyond on key elements of discipleship. I was able to affirm both his teaching ability and his writing ability and call him to greater levels of influence.

Use strength assessments. Strength Finders is one of our favorite strength assessments. While in the beautiful country of Croatia, we had everyone on our international leadership team take the Strength Finders assessment. After each person completed the assessment, we were able to process and figure out how each person's strengths contributed to the team. The impact was huge as team members grew in their understanding of each other as well as in how to use their area of strengths to grow their leadership.

Another great assessment is the Enneagram. The Enneagram is growing in popularity because it is multilayered and gives deeper understanding of both your strengths and weaknesses. Nancy Beach, leadership coach and author, writes, "The Enneagram is a tremendous tool for leadership and team relationships. Many teams have discovered how helpful the Enneagram can be for understanding those we work with—and those we live with!"[10]

We've taken both of these strength assessments and highly recommend them. They are valuable not only for personal understanding but also to help you understand your team more fully. As you grow in your understanding of how God has wired you as a leader, your influence will grow as well.

Leadership Is a High Calling

The bottom line is that leadership is a high calling and comes with some hefty responsibilities. Of all the obligations you carry, knowing your people and shepherding them to reach their greatest potential is high on God's agenda.

QUESTIONS TO ASK YOUR TEAM

1. What is one frustration you are experiencing in your position?
2. What would make your role here more rewarding?
3. What part of your job description brings you the most joy and fulfillment?
4. What is a dream that you would like to see realized here in our company during the next year?
5. What can I do to help you reach your goals?
6. What results do you expect to see?
7. Where are you experiencing the most stress in your job?
8. How are you feeling about the balance between work and home life at this time?
9. What do you feel we should stop doing that is no longer working?
10. What do I need to do to communicate more clearly?

QUESTIONS FOR SELF-LEADERSHIP

1. List the names of your team members, their spouses, and their children.

2. List three strengths of each team member.

3. Do you give members of your team the opportunity to share personally with you?

4. What part does hurry play in your daily schedule?

5. Describe one area of growth for each member of your team.

6. Take a few moments and pray for each member of your team.

4

Give the Gifts of Trust and Empowerment

In the long run empowerment should be a part
of every leader's toolkit. It strengthens everyone
in the organization, it keeps the company on the
path to success, and it builds one of the most
important elements on any team—trust.

—Colin Powell

Key: Listen to empower, not control.

One of my (Becky) favorite airlines is Southwest. I love
the boarding process. It's so orderly and the flight attendants are usually very pleasant and have big smiles.

Often, they're funny and entertaining. In fact, I once saw a flight attendant do a complete dance while demonstrating how to put on a life vest. The entire plane gave him a round of applause! I'm not alone; Southwest was listed by *Entrepreneur* as one of the top ten most empowering companies to work for in the United States.

We define empowering as:

> **Freeing others to take initiative and make decisions to enhance service and performance of the company or nonprofit.**

Leaders who are empowering don't need to control every decision. They trust their team members and encourage them to make choices that will enhance the company.

I recently heard Kimberly Greiner, the manager of community engagement for Southwest Airlines, speak about the values that drive the company. Famous for customer service and friendliness, Southwest has a unique company culture. In order to get hired, you have to demonstrate their three core values: a warrior spirit, a servant's heart, and a fun-loving attitude. They take customer service very seriously and empower their employees to go the extra mile to make customers happy.[1]

Empowering culture starts at the top. Gary Kelly, Southwest's president, values connection with his employees, and he has learned that the secret to great leadership is to listen so that his team feels valued. Connection builds trust. Kelly's employees trust his leadership, and in return he trusts them to take care of customer service. Kelly empowers his team by listening to his team members and encouraging them to make decisions that will benefit the company. He is known throughout the company for taking the time to listen and remember the stories of those who work for Southwest Airlines. As a result, his employees feel heard, valued, and empowered to be the best they can be for the greater good of Southwest Airlines.

What's the Big Deal about Empowerment?

You might be wondering, *Why is it so important to empower your team anyway?* To many leaders, empowering can feel awfully close to losing control, and that can feel downright scary! You worked hard to climb the corporate ladder, you're the expert, and you may feel the organization rises and falls on your abilities.

The truth is, "no one leads an organization to success alone."[2] Any thriving company, church, or community is rooted in the collective excellent effort of many. It's an easy mistake for leaders to take too much responsibility and believe that success depends upon them. If you go too far down the road of thinking that you alone are responsible for success, you'll become like the tyrannical ruler described in Proverbs 28:16 who comes to ruin. The bottom line is your team is vital to your success, and empowering is a win for everyone.

Empowering makes you more like Jesus. Jesus was the greatest leader of all time. Yet when you look at who was on His "go team," one could argue He could have picked a much stronger team. Most of His team was a bunch of school dropouts who became fishermen. Yet Jesus gave them the gift of trust and empowerment. At one point in His ministry, Jesus sent them out two by two (Mark 6:7) and gave them authority. Were they ready? From a human perspective, one could argue they weren't. From God's perspective, they were sent with His blessing. At the end of His ministry, after some of them had denied Him, fled from Him, and doubted His resurrection, Jesus once again gave them power and told them to go and make disciples of all nations (Matthew 28:19). In other words, "Go change the whole world!" Check out the rest of the story in the New Testament book of Acts.

If you're a person of faith claiming to love Jesus, follow His example and trust your team with authority. Then check in with them. Don't leave them abandoned, but definitely give them the gift of trust and empowerment.

Empowering demonstrates your ability to listen and add value. When you trust others and take time to consider their ideas, you show that you care not only about the profit of the company but also about the value of the person sharing the idea. The greatest leaders are those who encourage and empower others to reach their fullest potential. Empowering leaders ask questions like, "What can I do to help this become a win for you?" and "How can I empower you to achieve your goals and become all that you desire to be?"

Empowering keeps your team motivated. Scott Seibert, professor of management and organizations in University of Iowa's Tippie College of Business, examined the research of more than 140 studies conducted since 1995 that included thousands of workers. Research consistently showed that workers who felt empowered by their employers were more productive and had higher morale than those who were not empowered.[3] Google is a great example of this.

Google has become a world leader for innovation and is one of the most thriving and productive companies of our time. It's not surprising that Google has gone to great lengths to provide an empowering and creative work environment for their employees. In fact, employees are invited to spend 20 percent of their working week on projects that interest them personally. Team members are allowed and encouraged to explore new methods of making Google a more effective company.[4] No wonder the company is thriving!

Empowering helps others to reach their greatest potential. While I (Steve) was the lead pastor of a church in the suburbs of Denver, our leadership team longed to see our people serving on the frontlines of our city's greatest needs. We knew that most people wouldn't listen to our message unless they saw us living it out in real life. Our church's mission statement was "to make disciples who live and love like Jesus." Our town of 103,000 people was rife with child homelessness, at-risk youth, underperforming students, unemployment, senior neglect, and drug/alcohol addiction. We believed that our people could make a profound difference for Christ if we could get them to look beyond the church walls and empower them to act.

So what did we do?

We constantly reminded our people about the broken places in our community and world. We encouraged them to think about how Jesus would respond. We provided them with easy entry points to get involved (like the church-sponsored food bank or holiday dinners for the homeless). We challenged them to listen to the voice of the Holy Spirit and respond in obedience to what they thought He was saying. Most significantly, we didn't tell our people what they could and couldn't do. We trusted them and gave them permission to do whatever God had put on their hearts. They only had to agree to abide by three simple rules:

1. Don't get in doctrinal or moral trouble.
2. Don't ask for money (we helped with start-up costs but needed them to plan on becoming self-sustaining).
3. It starts and ends with you (in other words, you can't give it back to the church when you're tired of doing it).

Over time, our church became *an incubator of spiritual entrepreneurialism.* All kinds of community-transforming ministries were launched by people in our church family. Some of these outreaches became independent nonprofits and spread far beyond our local community. Our cancer-care ministry became nationally recognized. Because of the high success rate of our student-mentoring programs, we were given the opportunity to teach Bible classes in public schools. Creative partnerships and joint initiatives were formed with sister churches, business leaders, and civic authorities. It was a wild ride! A few old-time members complained that our church was "out of control." They were right. A movement had been birthed that spread to many of the other churches in our town. As we learned to trust and empower our people with doing ministry, amazing things happened. Lives were changed, and our community was powerfully impacted by the Gospel.

As you read that, I wonder what your reaction was. Did you think, *That guy is nuts! That would never work in my company or church!* Or maybe you thought, *That sounds completely out of control. I can't do that!* Or maybe you're intrigued and wondering, *What kind of impact could my company or church have if I empowered my team or congregation?*

What Exactly Does It Look Like for *You* to Empower?

Begin with trust. *Trust* is a small word with huge implications. It can feel very scary to many leaders. Trust raises questions like, "Do I have confidence in my team? Can I trust them to stay on board with the vision of our organization and move it forward?" Building trust takes intentionality but is worth every ounce of effort you put forth.

- **Trust begins with *you*.** Harvard business professor Amy Cuddy researched how leaders can make a positive first impression. She discovered that people subconsciously ask themselves two questions as soon as they meet you: "Can I trust this person?" and "Can I respect this person?" In her book *Presence*, Cuddy writes that human beings value trust so highly that only after trust is established does a person consider getting to know us further.[5] This has huge implications for us as leaders. If people can't trust you, they certainly won't follow you. Ask yourself, *Can my team members trust me? Do I keep my promises? Am I clear in my communication, and do I stay engaged?* One of the most effective ways to build trust is to be willing to admit when you're wrong and make amends. As team members see you take responsibility for your mistakes, they will own their mess-ups as well. Courageous leaders are willing to say, "I'm sorry. I was wrong. Will you forgive me?"

- **Trust your team members but verify actions.** Even though you give the gift of trust, you need to check back to be sure assignments have been completed. Too many leaders are all about the vision, and they become bored when there's not a new adventure on the horizon. As a result, they disengage. Or they feel inadequate—problems feel too big and challenges too great—so they simply procrastinate and end up checking out. This is a mistake. Trust your team but verify and stay engaged. In the absence of strong leadership there is always another who is ready to step in and take over.

Model and reward risk-taking. When our kids were little, we lived in Phoenix and had a pool in our backyard. Steve wanted to build into our son Josiah (JJ) the value of risk-taking. I (Becky) can still see our son standing by the side of the pool at eighteen months and Steve standing in the pool saying, "Jump, JJ, jump!" JJ would only hesitate a second, and then he would fly through the air and land with a splash in Steve's arms. Then Steve would move back a foot or two and again instruct JJ to jump! What was Steve doing? He was encouraging our son to take a risk, and he was building trust. Even at JJ's young age, Steve saw leadership skills and knew he needed to nurture risk-taking so that our son could grow up to be the leader he is today.

The same holds true in the workplace. People have a tendency to want to play it safe. That's understandable. But here's the thing: **There is no growth without risk.** Every new idea involves a risk. Every new initiative involves a risk. Even faith itself is a risk. The wise leader will both encourage risk and model it so that the organization continues to grow. Learn to respond to new and innovative ideas with the phrase "Try it."

There is nothing more discouraging to a team member than hearing "That will never work" or "We've tried that before and here's the problem." Management expert Peter Drucker said, "It's easier for companies to come up with new ideas than to let go of old ones."[6] You might have tried an idea before, or even several times, but this might be the magic moment when success arrives. So model and reward risk-taking, and be willing to let go of old ways of doing things.

What if in each staff meeting you asked, "What risk was taken this week?" What if you then gave out rewards (movie tickets, Starbucks gift cards, gift cards for dinner out) to the risk-takers? Imagine how innovative your company would become. Never undervalue a great risk!

Create an atmosphere of safety. Reading that you might be thinking, *Isn't that the opposite of risk-taking?* It's actually not. Within a culture of safety, team members can feel comfortable taking risks. How do you create a culture of safety?

- **Allow team members to pitch new ideas.** Every new idea brought to the table should be given value and treated with respect. Reward fresh ideas. It can be tempting for more senior employees to make younger members of an organization feel as though they haven't earned the right to speak or as though their ideas are foolish. This is a big mistake. It is often the younger members of the team that bring the most innovative ideas to the table.

- **Give team members permission to fail.** Don't shame failure; instead, reframe it as an opportunity for growth. Ask, "What can we learn from this?" Affirm the effort to try something new.

Tear down walls of mistrust between departments. Rebuilding broken trust is tricky business. Once credibility is lost, it's very tough to regain. It's not impossible, but it's challenging, and there needs to be a willingness on both sides for trust to be reestablished. Attentive listening rebuilds broken trust.

When trust has been fractured between departments, bring the key people together and bring the issues out in the open. Listen for the elephant in the room and what is not being spoken. Give permission for everyone to lay their concerns authentically on the table. Then lead everyone together to brainstorm about what it looks like to rebuild trust. Set ground rules: Everyone will honor and listen to each other. No one will interrupt. Sarcasm will not be allowed. Apologies will be expected and amends made. Broken trust can only be rebuilt with clear communication. Remember, 80 percent of communication is listening.

Another way to rebuild trust between departments is to celebrate the differences. Not every department has to function in exactly the same way. Diversity can be a blessing. Strive for synergy not sameness.

Clarify expectations. When people are unclear about expectations, they feel lost. Clear communication is always the best way to empower people; when your communication is clear, people trust you. When team members are clear on expectations, they can move forward with confidence and courage.

Our son-in-law Zach has experienced this in the navy. The military pushes empowerment and trust to a whole new level. I (Becky) remember when our son-in-law was deployed for the first time. As my daughter watched the ship go out to sea, she realized it was her husband, Zach, who was driving the ship. Zach was in his young twenties at the time.

Every night at sea during Zach's deployment, the commanding officer drafted nighttime orders and then went to bed. How in the world could you rest knowing you had left the entire ship under the watch of very young sailors? The reason the captain could trust his team was because he knew his orders were clear. As Brené Brown writes in *Dare to Lead*, "Clear is kind."[7]

Empower team members to strategize. Strategy is often set by executives, but it might best be set by the people on the ground doing the work. A great example of this is Apple. The executives have learned that the geniuses at the genius bar really *are* the experts. (And I [Becky] gotta say, I love those geniuses! They have helped me out without making me feel stupid more times than I can say.) Apple's mandate has been, "We hire people who tell *us* what to do, not the other way around."[8] That may feel like a scary way to run an organization, but there's benefit to team members feeling as though they can make decisions. There's a lot of truth to this quote from Bono: "Real leadership is when everyone else feels in charge."[9]

Focus on personal growth and raising the next generation of leaders. As leaders, the growth and well-being of the organization is often at the top of our priority list. But leadership calls us to focus on the personal growth of our team members and helping them to achieve their fullest potential. The greatest legacy you will leave will be those you have empowered to rise to their full potential. Together with each team member, write out a growth plan and keep a written record so the growth plan can be revisited.

A Closing Story

I (Steve) recruited Kyle to join my leadership team a few years after the Lord delivered him from a life of drugs and running from God. Kyle had hit bottom, but shortly after surrendering his life to Christ, he jumped in with both feet and headed off to seminary. That's where I met him. I was immediately drawn to the young leader and could see that he had a ton of potential for the kingdom. After a round of interviews with the leadership team, I offered him a full-time position as our high school pastor.

A year later, I promoted him to lead our entire student ministries department. That's when I started meeting every week with Kyle. On Tuesday mornings, we stuffed ourselves with bacon as we talked about the important issues of life and ministry. Kyle was a sponge. To develop his teaching skills, I started having him preach for me a few times a year. Kyle excelled. Between services, I coached him on what to do differently in the second service. Kyle was an eager and receptive learner. He took my advice and grew to become a very powerful communicator.

Pretty soon, Kyle was sharing almost half of the preaching load with me. His next step was to become our associate pastor. In that role, Kyle got immersed in church finance, strategic planning, and staff management. For four years, I poured my life into this young leader. During that time, Kyle was offered some other opportunities at much larger churches, but he hung in there with me.

In time, it became clear that Kyle was ready to move into the fullness of his ministry potential. That meant only one thing: Kyle needed to be the lead pastor. I needed to step aside and promote him into my role. Our last six months together were sweet. I poured everything I had into Kyle. He asked tons of questions about life and ministry. We prayed together, wept together, and laughed together. I'll never forget the day when I stood before the congregation and told them that they should invite Kyle to be my successor. A thousand-member church cast their votes. It was a unanimous yes. Today, Kyle is the thriving pastor of a growing church.

I saw potential in Kyle. As a leader, it was my responsibility to draw that potential out. One of the greatest rewards of my ministry life was handing the church over to a leader that I'd mentored and poured my life into.

There is always a risk to giving away power. The flip side is that there is too much at stake not to give the gift of trust and empowerment. It's a risk worth taking because giving the gift of trust and empowerment might just be the greatest investment of your life.

Tips for Emerging Leaders

Some of you are in the emerging leadership category, and you might be wondering why you are overlooked for greater positions of influence. After reading the story about Kyle, you might be wondering, *Why don't my leaders see my potential?* Is it possible that you are sabotaging your own advancement? Before we get to the reflective questions, here are a few tips for those of you who feel you are being overlooked.

Often older, more experienced leaders write off young emerging leaders because of their age. They assume they fit the stereotype of the typical millennial—self-centered, narcissistic, indulgent, and lazy.

We've listened to leadership of organizations and non-profits, coaching clients, and managers who are having difficulty with the millennials on their staff. For example, a project nurse overseeing a staff of younger nurses confided recently that the clinic where she works had to let go of several millennial nurses because they had, in her words, "a spirit of entitlement." They were known to cut corners, want more money, and have a critical spirit. Some of you who are older and reading this are nodding your head in agreement. But some of you who are in the millennial age group are protesting, saying, "That's not true of me!" We don't want to offend you. But we do want to challenge you to overcome the stereotypes that have been assigned to your generation. How do you do that? We have a few suggestions.

- Learn to ask for help—and listen to the answers.
- Affirm the leaders above you—don't become known as the critic or the cynic.
- Be teachable—ask how you can improve in your job performance. Listen and put into action the suggestions you receive.
- Stay focused on the job you are given and work hard to excel—even when no one is looking.
- Never talk behind a co-worker's back—listen for the positive and focus on that.
- Don't go on social media during work hours. (Unless that's your job.) Instead, become known as being a diligent worker.
- Ask someone older and more experienced to mentor you. When you meet with your mentor, be prepared with questions that will help you understand the concept of leadership more fully.
- If you're not in charge of it, don't stress over it. Stay in your lane.
- Be committed to personal growth. Ask others to help you assess your strengths and weaknesses.
- Go slow at offering others advice or suggestions. **Instead, listen more and speak less.**

QUESTIONS TO ASK YOUR TEAM

1. What does it look like for you to win in your current role? What can I do to help you accomplish that win?

2. What are your suggestions for strategy on that issue?

3. What's your idea for how to solve this problem?

4. How is your morale this week?

5. What ideas do you have to help with our customer service?

6. Which team member do you feel has made the most significant contribution in the past week?

7. As we hire people, what do you feel are the "must-haves" for our company?

8. Where do you see yourself in five-plus years?

9. Where do you need to take a risk to accomplish the next big success?

10. What do you need from me in terms of communication to help you feel more connected?

QUESTIONS FOR SELF-LEADERSHIP

1. What scares you most about giving up control?

2. How engaged are you on a scale from 1–10, 1 being burned out and not engaged and 10 being excited and all in?

3. Do you have a hard time giving credit to others? Similarly, do you feel the need to be affirmed constantly for "wins" in the company?

4. Do you take responsibility for your own actions, or are you quick to shift blame?

5. How comfortable are you allowing others to make decisions without you?

6. Have you broken any promises (or perceived promises) to your staff recently?

7. Think back to a time when you were under someone else's leadership and you felt empowered. What specifically made you feel that way?

5

Discern Hidden Values

The most important thing in communication is to hear what isn't being said.

—Peter Drucker

> **Key:** Ask great questions and listen to discern hidden values.

Every individual and every organization operates according to an internal set of beliefs and virtues. These are our values. They are the convictions that we consider to be of highest importance. Someone once said that values are the censors of our thoughts and the chaperones of our actions. Our values may be conscious or unconscious. They may be stated or unstated. They may be overt or obscure. They may be celebrated or suppressed, but every person and every community is driven by a discernable set of core values. A wise leader seeks to discover the hidden core values of each member of his or her team and how those values integrate with the collective values of the organization. Discerning underlying beliefs and driving motivations takes active listening—listening to what's being said and what's not being said.

When we first tipped our toes into the world of non-profit leadership, none of the leadership gurus were talking about values. Then the '90s hit. That's when, in the words of Patrick Lencioni, "The core values fad swept through corporate America like chicken pox through a kindergarten class."[1] Authors Jim Collins and Jerry Porras sold a million books convincing all of us that every business needed to have clearly articulated and frequently communicated core values if it wanted to move from good to great or be built to last. Everyone was suddenly into core values. The infatuation with core values wasn't misdirected. Core values matter. When defined and enforced, they shape corporate culture, guide decision-making, and clarify uniqueness. Clearly articulated and fully owned values:

- Express what matters
- Provide direction and boundaries
- Attract high-level talent
- Help people accept organizational change

- Play a key role in maintaining morale
- Become the compass that the organization uses to select staff and reward performance

Ken Boa says that "the first step in effective leadership is defining core values. Until that is done, the ship the leader is trying to steer has no rudder."[2] He's right. It's nearly impossible to define vision, strategy, and desired outcomes until there is clarity on core values.

When we stepped into the church we pastored in Denver, we immediately recognized the need to define the core values of our congregation. We knew that to discern the values of our people, we needed to listen to them. Surveys are a great way to glean what people are thinking and solicit their input, so we started by asking fifteen hundred of our people to respond to this question: "When and how did you experience the most growth in your spiritual journey?" The answers clearly fell into three categories. Some responded, "When I went through a crisis and people in the church were there for me." The second most common answer was, "When someone put an arm around my shoulder and showed me what it looked like to follow Jesus." The third was, "When I gave my life away in service to others." Interestingly, only six people said, "When I heard a great sermon." (Maybe that says something about my preaching?) After sifting through all of the responses to the survey, our leadership landed on three core values: mentoring, community, and mission. Our values were memorable, clear, and easy to explain. Even though that sounds neat and clean, it wasn't. At various times, a member of our staff would get passionate about something else and try to refocus the church in a different direction. While that focus might have been noble and well-intentioned, we needed to keep everyone aligned around our core values. That's where listening to discern unspoken values is critical.

When I (Steve) became the president of our mission agency, there was a burst of fresh excitement and anticipation. One of my first acts was to facilitate a conversation about values. On our website, we had posted a grocery list of fifteen to twenty cookie-cutter core values. No one had looked at them in ages. I'm not sure anyone (other than our webmaster) even knew that we had them.

I pulled together a task force of key staff, longtime members, and current board members to help us land on our core values. Together we rehearsed and scrutinized the history of our organization since its inception eight decades earlier. We sought to discern the motivations of our founding fathers and the convictions that they embedded in our DNA. (Back then, no one talked about core values.) After we'd clearly identified the beliefs and virtues that characterized our founders, we looked at the transformational events and catalytic leaders that forever altered the ethos and direction of our organization. Over its eighty-seven-year history, our organization had been influenced by a number of key events and visionary thinkers that changed how we related to one another and how we engaged with the outside world. For example, the fall of the Berlin Wall changed our organization profoundly. After the wall fell, we leaped at the opportunity to enter the former Soviet Union. As a result, we went from being a tight-knit community with everyone living in close proximity to one another to a global organization with staff located all over the planet. The fall of the wall forever altered the ethos of our organization.

As our team discussed core values, I instructed them to come up with only a handful; any more than a critical few wouldn't be helpful. After a lengthy process of give and take, we landed on these four core values:

- Bold faith
- Life-giving community
- Empowered partnership
- Strategic innovation

Everyone was pleased that we'd arrived at consensus around our core values. Everyone agreed that our organization was going to be rooted and defined by our four values. These values would set the culture of our organization. They would be the foundation upon which our vision would be built. They would be the litmus test for hiring staff and the filter through which every major decision would be made.

Twelve months later, the wheels started coming off. Turns out that while we thought we were fully aligned . . . we really weren't. Everyone had memorized our four core values and could readily spout them off, but we weren't on the same page. While everyone agreed on the overall direction, we had conflicting ideas and competing priorities on how we were going to get there. We were like a giant iceberg. Everyone subscribed to the values that were on top of the waterline, but what was underneath was threatening to sink the ship. When we reviewed our four core values, it quickly became apparent that we weren't all speaking the same language. While everyone had enthusiastically embraced the values that we'd outlined, each of us had different interpretations of what those values meant.

As we listened carefully and began to dig in to the issues, it became apparent that we were not all with one another on how we defined key words like *partnership* and *innovation*. It also became apparent that all of us on the leadership team were being motivated by a set of deeply cherished personal values that had never made it to the surface. These unstated and unconscious values had begun to threaten and derail our vision.

While I valued individual freedom, key leaders on my team valued control. While I valued rapid growth, some on the leadership felt slower growth was easier to manage. While I valued risk-taking, others valued safety. It wasn't a matter of right versus wrong. The problem was that we weren't aligned. We hadn't taken enough time to listen to one another and to draw out of each other the thoughts, perceptions, and beliefs that lay beneath the surface of our words. You see, it's one thing to identify values; it's another to clarify their meaning. Both steps are important. Identifying and clarifying values is not a simple, one-step process. Like a fine wine, it takes time. Ideas have to simmer. It's a process that requires intentionality, concentration, and genuine curiosity.

Wisdom and Values

Solomon understood the trickiness of discerning hidden values. He encouraged his son with these words: "Tune your ears to wisdom, and concentrate on understanding. Cry out for insight, and ask for understanding. Search for them as you would for silver; seek them like hidden treasures" (Proverbs 2:2–4 NLT). In another passage, Solomon wrote, "The purposes of a person's heart are deep waters, but one who has insight draws them out" (Proverbs 20:5).

Detecting and respecting the unspoken motivations and assumptions of those around you takes wisdom, insight, and understanding. You have to put in the effort to dig beneath the surface. It requires attentiveness, concentration, and genuine curiosity.

Jesus and Values

Jesus understood the importance of core values. In His Sermon on the Mount, the Master Leader outlined the values that would characterize His followers (Matthew 6:1–34). Top on the list of Jesus' core values was pleasing the Father. In Matthew 22:37, Jesus put it this way: "You must love the LORD your God with all your heart, all your soul, and all your mind" (NLT). In his book *The Perfect Leader*, Ken Boa describes the first and greatest commandment as "the prism through which all other values must shine; the filter through which all of life's choices are made and solutions are drawn."[3] The second core value of Jesus was loving others. He put it this way in Mark 12:31: "'Love your neighbor as yourself.' There is no commandment greater than these." Jesus had other values that He wanted to embed in the DNA of His followers, but these two values were at the very top: love God and love others. If you follow Jesus, then those two need to be at the top of your core value list. Loving God and loving others is all about listening. Listening to God. Listening to others. When you listen, you place value on others. You show that you care about what they think and feel. When you listen well, you love well . . . and you lead better.

Keeping the Team Aligned

Keeping teams aligned around a defined set of core values is difficult at best. That's in part because there are different kinds of values that constantly come to the surface.

- **Some values are actual while other values are aspirational.** There's a big difference between what is and what we hope will be. There's a place for both kinds of values, but the difference needs to be noted. When discerning collective values, it's important to ask, "Is this an actual value or an aspirational value?" Listening to how your team members respond to that question will quickly reveal whether the value is actually present and owned or simply desired.

- **Some values are historic while other values are current.** To a very significant extent, the corporate values of an organization reflect the personal values of its founder. The more time and distance from the founder, the greater the drift from those founding values. When discerning collective values, it's important to ask, "To what extent are the values of our founder still in our DNA?"

- **Some values are primary while other values are secondary.** Sifting out secondary values from primary values can be immensely challenging! Some values are worth dying for. Other values, while still important, can be compromised or modified. When discerning collective values, it's important to ask, "Is this a value worth going to the mat for?"

- **Some values are personal while other values are organizational.** Aligning personal values with corporate values is an ongoing process. As a leader in your organization, it's important to become acutely aware of your own personal values and how those values relate and integrate with the collective values of the organization you serve.

All Values Need Definition

In our organization, I came to realize that while we all agreed on certain values, our definitions for those values were different. Those differences were creating problems for us.

As we began the rugged task of bringing greater alignment to our teams, there were three important lessons that I learned:

Lesson #1: If you're going to lead your team in identifying and clarifying core values, you'd better be in touch with your own values. Most of us who are action-oriented leaders have a hard time defining what we value and articulating those values to our team members. If we're going to lead well, we need to understand and appreciate the motivations and convictions that drive us and predispose us toward making certain decisions. We need to understand that our personal values are made up of everything that has happened to us, including the influences of our parents, our religious beliefs, our education, reading, experiences, and more. As leaders, we need to listen to our own hearts. We need to get in touch with what inspires and ignites us.

Consider this list of values:

Ambition, freedom, individuality, diversity, equality, integrity, responsibility, accuracy, respect, teamwork, excellence, influence, challenge, friendliness, discipline, generosity, flexibility, persistence, competency, faith, family, loyalty, honesty, risk-taking, innovation, security, independence, optimism, change, compassion, learning, empowerment, collaboration, dedication.

ASK YOURSELF THESE QUESTIONS:

- What are the top three values on this list that are most important to you? You'd probably argue that you value everything on this list, but it's the cream at the top that really matters.
- How do you most often respond to change, challenge, or chaos? How you answer this question says a lot about what you truly value.
- What kinds of books do you like to read and what kinds of TV shows do you like to watch? What does your answer to this question say about your personal values?

Recently, a young leader that I (Steve) am mentoring asked me, "What process did you use to discover and define your personal values?" As we talked, it became clear to me that he was seeking to get in touch with his own values. I wish I could have told him that it was a simple three-step process. But I landed on my personal values after much self-reflection and comparing and contrasting my impulses with those of others. Self-discovery is a process that takes time, intentionality, concentration, and genuine curiosity.

Over the years, I've compiled a working list of beliefs and cherished qualities that shape my thinking and predispose me to certain actions and outcomes. For example, I believe that making disciples of Jesus is the end-game of life. I believe that local churches are the world's best hope.

I believe that people thrive when they're free to pursue their own dreams and callings. I believe that growth is good and change is positive. These beliefs, or core values, influence every decision I make. Obviously, I recognize and affirm that my convictions aren't shared by everyone else. Good people have different beliefs and priorities. They value different things. While I value the qualities of flexibility, positivity, and individual freedom, others value structure, realism, and control. All of us are shaped by our past experiences and by the uniqueness of our own personalities. It's not that one set of values is right and the other is wrong. All have their place. What's important is that each of us is in touch with our own personal values and aware of how we interject those values into our relationships and decision-making.

Lesson #2: The personal values of your team members will meld to form your corporate culture. Wise leaders take the time and initiative to listen to and understand the personal values of their team members. They know that each of their staff brings personal values into the workplace. They understand that the experiences, beliefs, and upbringings of their team members merge together to form corporate culture. That's why wise leaders passionately pursue "knowing." They ask personal questions that uncover motivations and bias. Questions like:

- What are your first impressions or feelings about this?
- Why do you think you feel so passionately about this issue?

- What part of your job do you think is most important?
- How would you describe a win in your job?
- What does a fail look like to you?

Drawing out the personal values of your staff requires time, intentionality, concentration, and genuine curiosity. In other words: active listening. The effort is worth it. As you draw out the personal values of your staff, you show them respect and honor their uniqueness. In that way, you're keeping in step with Jesus' second core value, "You shall love your neighbor as yourself."

When staff members share answers, look for the telling signs of body language. As Solomon said, "A glad heart makes a happy face" (Proverbs 15:13 NLT). You can learn a lot by looking at faces! In many of the team meetings I host, I assign a team member to help me assess the body language of the participants. I can get so wrapped up in leading the conversation and pushing through the agenda that I miss the subtle cues that can indicate disagreement or confusion.

Lesson #3: Core values become accessible when they're clearly defined. It's critically important to be as clear, concise, and specific as possible.

One very helpful way to drill down into the meaning of your core values is to compose value statements. Value statements are precisely worded assertions that convey definition and meaning. They describe actions that flesh out core values. For example, it's one thing to say that you value customer service, but a value statement takes it a step further to say, "We will respond to all of our emails within twenty-four hours," or, "Every phone call will be answered by the third ring." It's one thing to say that you value adaptability, but a value statement says, "Once a decision has been made, we will adjust to the best of our ability without whining."

In his book *Sticky Teams*, Larry Osborne, the Pastor of North Coast Church in San Diego, noted that the most powerful tool he'd discovered for ensuring staff alignment in values and decisions is what he calls plumb lines. Osborne says that plumb lines are "organizational proverbs" or "pithy sayings that describe clearly and concisely what we value."[4] Osborne has a list of ten plumb lines that he shares with his pastoral staff to clarify expectations and priorities. An example of one plumb line is this: "Real ministry takes place in small groups."[5] The staff at North Coast discussed this plumb line and came up with a further explanation stated this way: "A crowd is not a church. It's impossible for the biblical 'one another's' to be lived out in a large group setting dominated by casual acquaintances. Therefore, the success of our ministry will be determined by the number of people we have in small groups, not the number of people who attend our weekend services."[6]

Just as plumb lines are used in construction to ensure that walls are straight, organizational plumb lines ensure that teams are aligned. With plumb lines, it's easy to identify misalignment as soon as it begins to happen. Well-worded value statements let everyone know what's expected and how their success will be measured. Here are a few questions that leaders need to ask:

- How would defining our plumb lines help us to align?
- In what areas do we need to define our plumb lines?
- Whom do we need on our team to help us define our plumb lines?

Lesson #4: Core values are worthless unless you put into play the practices that sustain them. It's hard to identify values, but it's even harder to live by them. As Patrick Lencioni writes, "Values inflict pain."[7] If they don't inflict pain, you probably don't take them seriously enough. Think about it. If you say you value physical fitness but you never work out hard enough to break a sweat, you probably don't value fitness. Sustaining values demands constant vigilance and reinforcement. It's not enough to post your core values on the lunchroom wall. You need to encourage practices that reinforce values.

One of our values is "bold faith." In order to sustain that value, we ask our staff to gather twice a day—at 11:00 a.m. and 2:00 p.m.—for a ten-minute prayer break. That's just one practice that we use to remind ourselves that our dependence is on the Lord. A simple prayer break refocuses our attention on the source of our trust and provision. Ask yourself and your teams:

- How do your direct reports exemplify our values?
- What daily practices can we instill that will reinforce our values?

- Where are we giving lip service to a value without really living it out?

It All Comes Back to Wisdom

Remember Solomon's pithy commands, "Tune your ears to wisdom, and concentrate on understanding" (Proverbs 2:2 NLT) and "The purposes of a person's heart are deep waters, but one who has insight draws them out" (Proverbs 20:5)? The process of getting wisdom and understanding can't be rushed. You need to "tune your ears." Listening well takes time, intentionality, and concentration. Slow down long enough to discover your own core values as a leader and then invest the time and effort in listening to draw out the personal values of your team members. Listen for what is said as well as what is not said. That will give you greater understanding into unspoken values. Only then will you be able to clearly define the plumb lines that will help to keep your team aligned.

═══ QUESTIONS TO ASK YOUR TEAM ═══

1. What values best describe our organization?
2. What should the plumb lines be that define those values?
3. Who in this company do you feel best exemplifies those values?

4. Moving forward, what needs to change for us to be aligned around those values?

5. How do our company values align with your personal values?

QUESTIONS FOR SELF-LEADERSHIP

1. Out of the list mentioned earlier in this chapter, which three values did you choose?

2. What made you choose those three?

3. Write a plumb-line paragraph defining each value you chose.

4. How do your personal values shape your leadership style?

5. How do your personal values shape the culture of your organization?

ADDITIONAL QUESTIONS TO DISCERN HIDDEN VALUES OF FELLOW TEAM MEMBERS

1. Do you consider yourself a rule-follower?

2. Do you crave adventure or get bored easily?

3. How important is tradition to you?

4. How important is personal autonomy to you?

5. Do you work better in a team or independently?

6. What do you do to inspire creativity?

7. What practices are a part of your faith journey?

8. What issues do you feel strongly about and why?

9. On a scale of 1–10, with 1 being not important at all to 10 being very important, how strongly do you value organization and order?

10. Do you consider yourself a detail person or more of a visionary?

11. Tell me about a book you've read recently.

12. Tell me what success will look like for that project.

13. What will be the measure points for a win?

14. Tell me about your single most important accomplishment.

15. How do you as a manager celebrate wins with your team?

16. How do you as a manager create safety for people to fail?

17. Tell me about a failure in your department and how that failure was handled.

18. What's one behavior in others that frustrates you?

19. When there's a conflict, what's your preferred method of communication?

20. What makes you feel "out of control"?

21. What activities do you enjoy and engage in regularly to relax?

22. How would those closest to you describe you?

23. Who is one of your heroes and why do you admire that person?

24. Whom do you envy and why?

25. What is one aspiration that you have put on hold in your life?

6

Invite Others to Help Shape Vision

> Truly remarkable leadership is not just about
> motivating others to follow, it's about inspiring
> them to become leaders themselves and setting
> the stage for even greater opportunity for future
> generations.
>
> —Condoleezza Rice

Key: Allow others to help shape the vision.

If you want your team to be "up" on your vision, you've got to get them "in" on it. Scripture says, "Plans succeed through good counsel; don't go to war without wise advice" (Proverbs 20:18 NLT). Solomon also opined, "Plans go wrong for lack of advice; many advisors bring success" (Proverbs 15:22 NLT).

There are two core skills that leaders need when creating and communicating organizational vision: **the ability to listen well** and **the ability to ask great questions.** People will only move to your position when they feel that you truly understand them. To feel truly understood, they need to feel heard. To feel heard, they need to see that you are genuinely interested in their advice and opinions. Drawing out thoughtful counsel from others is a powerful and necessary leadership art. As the wise man said, "Though good advice lies deep within the heart, a person with understanding will draw it out" (Proverbs 20:5 NLT).

A few years ago, I was chairing a meeting that was filled with over twenty key leaders. The goal of the meeting was to create a bias for change and foster alignment around organizational direction. The room was loaded with strong personalities, strident opinions, and long-standing hurts. I needed this band of independent individualists to understand and embrace the reality that they needed to come together as a team in order to address the critical challenges that the organization was facing. But first, I needed a way to defuse the tension that lay just below the surface of congeniality. To set the tone for a free-flowing conversation, I began by sharing a silly little poem that I'd quickly composed a few hours before the meeting.

> There once was a German beer maker who crafted a
> brew.
> His business caught on and rapidly grew.

He needed more staff to fill out his crew,

but high in the mountains, workers were few.

So, he opened employment offices in far distant
    lands

that sent down laborers to help with his plans.

With more employees to help his business expand,

he opened more outlets to feed the demand.

Soon his beer became a famed brand

and he had offices and outlets all over the land.

Everything flourished when he was the boss,

but when he retired there was a great loss.

Without a firm leader holding things tight,

everyone did as he deemed right.

The employment offices stopped hiring and crafted
    beers of their own.

The distribution outlets stopped selling and set a
    new tone.

The offices and outlets took over control,

which left the plant staff with no leadership role.

In time, the brand was hopelessly diluted

and trust between workers completely uprooted.

The workers quit working and profits declined.

The debt ratios rose and more leaders resigned.

A dozen years later, the company failed.

The beer maker's vision completely derailed.

After the laughter over my incomparable poetic skill had
subsided, I asked the team this question: "What does the

tale of the German beer maker say to us?" The answer was immediate: "We need to drink a lot more beer!"

That lighthearted moment released the tension in the air and set the tone for an open and honest conversation about the situation in which we'd found ourselves.

Create a Bias for Change

Knowing that the first task of a leader is to define reality, I followed up the silly poem with a PowerPoint presentation that described the characteristics of an organization in the various stages of its life cycle. "Where do you think this organization is at?" I asked. I put up a slide that described the traits of a business that had passed its peak and was headed into decline.

Signs of an Organization in Decline

- Control reverts to a few
- Commitment to outdated strategies
- Frequent staff and volunteer turnover
- Proliferation of formal procedures
- Lack of excitement and passion
- Inability to address key challenges
- Internal conflict and distrust
- Crisis-oriented planning
- Growing isolation and irrelevance

Then I asked, "Do you see any of these characteristics in our organization?" As key leaders and board members alike evaluated the list, heads began to nod around the room. Reality was beginning to dawn. The team had to embrace the hard truth if they were ever going to rally around a new vision.

Having been around the block a few times, I knew that simply sharing the raw data wasn't enough to create a powerful bias for change. I broke our leaders into small groups and asked each group to come up with five reasons as to why the finance and membership numbers were trending down. Once a list of reasons was on the whiteboard, I asked the team to share with one another how they were feeling. Listening to each other was painful but redemptive. We now had the necessary bias for change. By the end of that meeting, the leaders were ready to consider a new vision for the future.

At the beginning of the next session, I asked the leaders to make a list of what they felt were the unique tools or value-adds that their organization had to offer. We narrowed that list down to the top ten tools.

I then asked the team, "What kind of legacy do you want to leave? What would it look like if you were wildly successful? What do you want this organization to be known for?" Throughout the morning, I repeatedly said, "This is what I think I hear you saying. Is that correct?"

After hours of listening to one another, the vision for a preferred future began to crystalize in all of our minds. By the time our mini-retreat had ended, everyone was feeling a fresh sense of purpose and hope. As we prepared to wrap up our last session, I asked everyone in the room to give a one-word description of how they were feeling. Positive and uplifting words filled the atmosphere in the room, words like *inspired, excited, eager, awed,* and *challenged.* During that mini-retreat, the leadership had turned a critical corner. There were still many challenges that lay before the team, but they had taken a powerful first step toward laying the foundation for an organizational rebirth.

Why Do Many Visions Fail?

Research tells us that 70 percent of organizational change efforts fail.[1] Why? The problem isn't with the vision. The problem is with communicating the vision and listening to get the buy-in of those who will be most affected. Only then will you be able to keep everyone aligned around the vision.

People don't want to be sold a vision. Casting a vision is one thing. Catching it is another. It's true that people won't buy in to your vision until they buy in to you. But even likability has its limits. Just because people like you doesn't mean they'll follow you when the really hard choices have to be made. If your people are going to have to spill their blood to see the vision realized, they've got to own it. In order to own it, they've got to have a role in creating it and feel like their ideas were heard. As I said earlier, if they're going to be up on the vision, they need to be in on the vision.

The more fingerprints on the vision and strategic plan, the greater the commitment and loyalty. A shared vision is always more powerful than a solitary vision. A shared vision will energize your team, build trust, and ensure long-term commitment.

Some executives think that a shared vision has to bubble up from the bottom rather than coming down from the top. They think that the leader's job is to facilitate the vision of others, rather than their own vision. On the surface, that sounds selfless and spiritual. But in reality that doesn't work. I tried it once and failed miserably.

In one of my previous leadership positions, I gathered a large number of people in the room and asked one question: "What's your vision for the future of our organization?" Dumb idea. I took all the bits and pieces from scores of people and tried to manipulate them into a comprehensive yet coherent vision. That was a bust. Giving voice to everybody and anybody is a huge mistake. It's like the airline pilot from a few years ago who got fired for polling his passengers on where to land the plane. Yup. It really happened. (Well maybe . . . I read about it on the internet.) Apparently, a wicked thunderstorm was lingering over the planned destination. The control tower warned the pilot about the potential for a rough landing and suggested an alternative airport in a nearby city. The captain of the plane couldn't make up his mind on what to do, so he sent the flight attendants through the cabin, scoring the votes of the passengers: "Newark in the storm, or Boston in the clear?" Can you believe it?! That's an incredible abdication of leadership. You might have platinum executive status with that airline, but I guarantee, if you heard a pilot polling the passengers on safety, you'd forsake your benefits and abandon that airline forever.

We're not saying to let everyone else set the vision. We are saying that people want their leader to lead. As the leader, you can't delegate vision. Articulate the dream, but then invite others to help shape the dream. You may know where you want your organization to go, but you need to invite the input and feedback of others. Include them in the shaping of the vision. Remember this: If they're in on it, they're far more likely to be up on it.

Igniting a Vision That Catches

Here's the approach that I've had the most success with when crafting and communicating a vision.

Step One: Identify Your Influencers

Do you know who your most powerful influencers are? How well do you know them? If you haven't taken the time to hear their stories and listen to their personal hopes and dreams, you'd better put off the vision-casting process until you do. These are the people who have the potential to make your vision a dream come true or turn it into *A Nightmare on Elm Street*. If your key influencers aren't on your leadership team, you've got another problem.

Step Two: Gather Their Thoughts

Don't rush to share your thoughts. Listen first. James said, "Be quick to listen, slow to speak" (James 1:19). Solomon put it this way: "Too much talk leads to sin. Be sensible and keep your mouth shut" (Proverbs 10:19 NLT). Start by meeting with a handful of your key influencers individually. Over lunch or a tall at Starbucks, ask them to give you their honest feedback on an issue or two. If all goes well and you sense that you're on a similar page, ask them if they'd be willing to join a "clearness committee" to help you discern and refine the future direction of your organization.

When you pull your clearness committee together, ask a set of open-ended questions like these:

- What do you think we truly value?
- What are we good at?
- What's in our organizational DNA and how did it get there?
- What were the critical inflection points in our organization? How did those inflection points change us?
- What are we uniquely positioned and equipped to do?

After you've asked each of these questions, shut up and listen. Really listen. Your key influencers must have your full attention. Take notes on what they say. Pay close attention to their body language. What makes them fidget or cross their arms? What lights up their faces? Make sure that everyone says something. Don't minimize or negate their thoughts and feelings. You can ask for clarification, but don't tell them what to think. After everyone has had a chance to provide some input, look over your notes and try to summarize what you've heard them saying. Thank them for their valuable insight and transparency. Let them know that you're going to go away and think about what they've said. Ask them if they'd be willing to meet again after you've had time to process their thoughts.

Step Three: Noodle on It

Individual reflection is a critical aspect of leadership. The busier I (Steve) get, the more time I need for it. For me, I think and pray at my best when I'm hiking in the mountains or sitting in an airplane seat listening to worship music on my noise-cancelling earbuds. What works best for you? During your think time, listen to your heart. What are you thinking and feeling? What lights you up? What weighs you down? How does what you're thinking and feeling resonate with the thoughts and feelings of your key influencers? Is there a common thread of purpose and longing? Listen to your heart, but don't just listen to yourself. Consider carefully the input from your people. Take the time to let it soak in. Let it stew. Let it simmer. Don't rush the vision-crafting process. As your thoughts and the thoughts of your clearness committee begin to congeal into a sense of common purpose and direction, summarize it in a statement with as few words as possible. Mull the statement over. Shorten it if you can. Be sure to keep it in draft form. Hold it loosely because it will probably change.

Step Four: Imagine Together

Pull your clearness committee together for a second round of questions. Now it's time to ask more forward-looking questions like, "What kind of legacy do we want to leave? What would it look like if we were wildly successful at what we do? What do we want to be famous for?" Listen to the hopes and dreams of your people. If and when it seems like everyone is tracking along the same lines of what you've been thinking and feeling, it's time to share what God has put in your heart. If you share it with sensitivity and invite your team to refine the idea, it won't come down as a mandate from the mountain, but as the result of a positive exercise in collective listening.

Be sure to read the body language of your team members. If you sense pushback or tension, stop and invite others to share what they're feeling. Allow them to ask questions that will help them clarify the vision in their thinking. Be willing to modify. Revise. Your people need to know that you value their input, are actively listening to them, and are more than willing to modify your vision to encompass the passions and desires of your team.

Step Five: Take It for a Test Run

Before you cast the vision in concrete to the many, test it on a few. Having gone through the process with your key influencers, you know they'll have your back. The early adopters are with you. Now you need to engage a broader circle of influence. Set up a handful of small-group meetings to begin unpacking the vision. Be sure to let people know that the vision isn't your idea alone. It's a shared vision. Ask for their input on how they see the vision unfolding and how it affects what they do. Again: Listen well. Ask clarifying questions. Look for body language. As you receive the initial impressions and insights of your people, write them down and promise to bring them back to your clearness committee.

Step Six: Explore Next Steps

After you've met with a few groups and heard their questions and concerns, it's time to pull your clearness committee together for another round of conversation. Begin by conveying the feedback that you've received. Discuss the questions and concerns. Then ask your team a set of questions like these:

- What kind of feedback have we received?
- Where is it coming from?
- Are there adjustments we can make to get more buy-in?
- Who are the critical stakeholders that have bought in to the vision?
- How can we leverage their influence as vision ambassadors?

- How do we proceed from here?
- Are we all in? If not, why not? What will it take to get there?

Step Seven: Deliver!

Now that you've got growing support for the vision among your principal stakeholders, it's time to go public. Whenever you share the vision, talk about how it benefits your people. Connect what you say to what's uppermost in the minds of your people: "How is this going to affect me?" Don't try to communicate the need for change by pointing solely to fact and figures. Your people need to know that you understand and appreciate their fears. During seasons of major organizational change, I make a habit of going from office to office, visiting with my staff. I ask them how they're doing with the changes. I want to know what they're thinking and feeling. Leaders need to know how the changes are impacting the lives of their people. By listening, you show that you care. By caring, you gain support and trust for the difficult changes that you need to make.

If you follow through on each of these seven steps, there's a strong likelihood that most of your people will hang with you when the high water comes. Because you've engaged them in crafting the vision, you've ignited their passions, gained their commitment, and earned their trust and loyalty. But what if you've gone through each of these steps and there's still a key leader who's holding out or skeptical of the vision? I've been there . . . many times.

Let's face it: Not everyone is going to buy in to the vision. With some folks, you just have to settle for getting permission. There will always be a moment in time when the debate has to stop and a decision has to be made. As the leader, you've got to figure out when that moment has come.

You've listened well. You've taken into account all the opinions and perspectives. Now it's time. Stop the debate. Make the decision. You might lose a few people who can't get on board with the vision. That's okay. Some people are better off moving on—it's in their best interest and yours.

A Few Closing Comments

As we close this chapter, we realize that you might be a mid-level leader reporting to a senior leader who isn't able to articulate a clear vision or sets a vision that you don't agree with. What should you do? You have several choices:

1. **If you can't support the vision of the leadership, you could leave honorably rather than causing dissension.** In the early 1980s we served under a leader who got stuck in the weeds and couldn't articulate a vision. Being a strong, risk-taking visionary, I (Steve) was getting more and more frustrated. The temptation for me would have been to cause dissension by campaigning for my own vision. But after we processed and prayed through our frustrations, we chose to quietly step down rather than cause dissension. The rule

of thumb is this: Always leave honorably. Don't sabotage your own credibility by trying to stir up others in your defense.

2. **You could meet with your boss and pitch a possible compromise.** If your boss loves the idea you've pitched, great! If not, you must be able to let it go and not create a rebellion.

3. **You could take the opportunity to invest in your own personal growth and development.** Perhaps for financial or other reasons you can't make the transition to another job. Rather than going to work frustrated each day, commit to growing in humility, grace, and patience. Make it a personal goal to learn as much as you can about styles of leadership to prepare for future positions. Your goal might be to grow in your own communication skills so that you're prepared for greater spheres of influence. With your own personal goals defined, turn every challenge into an opportunity to grow.

Vision is crucial to a thriving organization. Spend time in prayer and personal reflection. Ask God to give you a compelling vision. If you're not the CEO, ask God to give you a compelling vision for your department or the projects that you oversee. Don't rush. Take the time to follow the steps we've outlined and you'll be successful in gathering a tribe who will support your vision with passion and a whole heart.

Questions for Your Team

1. Do you have a vision statement for your life? If so, what is it?

2. What is your next step toward accomplishing that vision?

3. Within the framework of our organization, where do you see yourself in three years?

4. Are you crystal clear on your current role and what your responsibilities are? What project are you working on at this time?

5. What are your top priorities for the next year?

6. What most often keeps you from achieving your goals?

7. Where do you see us making the most headway toward our vision?

8. What do you see as the major hurdles to accomplishing the vision?

9. Do you have ideas on the vision that you have not yet had the opportunity to share?

10. What are your ideas to bring people into greater alignment with the vision?

QUESTIONS FOR SELF-LEADERSHIP

1. Can you clearly articulate the vision?

2. Do you understand the cost for accomplishing the vision?

3. Is there something you need to communicate more clearly in order to get alignment on the vision?

4. What is the greatest risk to moving forward with the vision?

5. How will you manage your own self-doubt when hurdles come that invite you to believe accomplishing the vision is impossible?

7

Engage Conflict Constructively

Conflict is an almost daily event in organiza
tional life. Wherever two or three are gathered,
one is likely to disagree!

—Lawrence W. Wilson

> **Key:** When in conflict, listen, manage
> your emotions, and stay curious
> to navigate it constructively.

In the vocational pools that I (Steve) swim in, conflict comes
with the territory. I live in a world of strong personalities
and lots of strident opinions. There are multiple-choice answers on many issues. As the president of a global nonprofit,

I've had to come to peace with conflict. Early in my ministry I feared it. Today, I view it as a friend.

We've all heard the cliché "conflict is inevitable." While we all know that, sometimes we need the reminder. Whenever you have people from different cultures, with different experiences, values, personalities, and opinions . . . you will have conflict. Studies show that up to 40 percent of a manager's day will be spent dealing with conflict.[1]

The paradoxes of organizational leadership are a breeding ground for tumbles and rumbles. Within every staff team, there are tensions to be managed:

- Optimism vs. reality
- Speed vs. quality
- People vs. projects
- Tough vs. tender
- Empowerment vs. accountability
- Caution vs. risk
- Focus vs. choice
- Vision vs. detail
- Short-term vs. long-term

The list goes on and on. Everyone brings their personal bias and perspectives into these tensions. Leadership teams will be all over the map. These paradoxes are virtually guaranteed to create conflict. Then there are the practical matters of salaries, recognitions, reviews, promotions, and management styles. There's a plethora of issues that can divide and undermine the unity of a team.

Effectively dealing with conflict may arguably be the hardest thing that you as a leader have to do. How you handle conflict will determine whether it works toward your team's advantage or your team's demise. How you respond to conflict will either build trust in your leadership or erode it.

We all know that conflict can be either constructive or destructive. Conflict is constructive when it makes high-functioning teams even more high performing. Conflict is a win when it results in growth, creative solutions, increased productivity, greater alignment, and the freedom to challenge the status quo. Conflict is destructive when it disintegrates into snarky emails, snippy comments, rolled eyes, and crossed arms. Conflict is destructive when it spirals down into paralysis, avoidance, polarization, negative morale, and a loss of productivity.

The outcome largely depends on how leadership navigates the rumble. The first step to navigation is to change the lens through which you view the conflict.

Changing the Lens through Which You View Conflict

Pastor and author Lawrence Wilson points out that most leaders approach conflict in one of two classic ways: conflict management or conflict resolution. Conflict management assumes that conflict is a constant feature of group life. Conflict resolution sees conflict as an interruption of normal life.[2]

With conflict management you merely try to contain conflict and keep it within boundaries. Conflict resolution pushes leaders to find a solution as soon as possible. In either case, conflict is seen as a battle. But when conflict is viewed as a battle, the options are either lose-lose or win-lose.

What if there's another option?

What if we viewed conflict as a playing field?

When viewed as an opportunity for transformation, conflict can be a win for everyone involved. In essence, conflict becomes the pathway to strengthen the life of the team and improve shared goals. But that takes intentionality on the part of the leader. Before we unpack how that best happens, take a minute and pause. Consider. What's your natural bent when dealing with conflict?

What's Your Natural Bent?

As we see it, there are basically five styles that we naturally revert to when facing conflict:

- Dominate
- Minimize
- Avoid
- Compromise
- Collaborate

Some of us were born to debate or compete. We thrive on conflict. As soon as tension surfaces, we dive into fight mode. We relish debate and vigorously assert our ideas. In the end, we want to win! The problem is that members on our team may see us as dominating and may feel intimidated by our assertiveness.

For others of us, the natural bent is to minimize. With this style of conflict management, we seek to play down differences, highlight commonalities, and celebrate peace as a way to defuse the tension in the room. We desperately want everyone to feel good and will do whatever it takes to achieve that goal. The problem with this style is that the core issues are never really dealt with.

The avoidance response is self-explanatory. Those of us with this natural bent hate conflict! Rather than directly engaging with the tension, we try to divert the focus onto something less polarizing. When arguments break out between staff, we excuse ourselves and get more coffee. But chronic conflict avoiders end up losing the respect of their staff.

Those who love compromise are all about give-and-take. Those with this natural bent expect that everyone on all sides of the conflict will be willing to give up something in order to get something. Difficulty arises here when the opposing party is not willing to compromise. We leave the discussion frustrated.

Finally, those of us with a bent toward collaboration are eager to pursue honest dialogue, examine differences, and seek mutually beneficial alternatives. This is the strongest approach to conflict and carries the most potential for transformation.

Which one of these approaches toward conflict is your natural bent? It's important to know your default response.

But it's also important to recognize that there's more than one way to deal with conflict. Each situation may require a different approach.

There is no one right way to deal with conflict. However, there are plenty of wrong ways to deal with it. Any of the following approaches will virtually guarantee a negative result:

- Ignoring it
- Blaming others for it
- Complaining about it
- Throwing temper tantrums or pouting
- Dropping hints without being direct (passive-aggressive)
- Being divisive by trying to recruit people for your point of view
- Gossiping about those who hold a different opinion

So how do you, as the leader, handle conflict in a way that makes it constructive and transformational? We are convinced that the key to healthy conflict is to listen well by managing your emotions, staying curious, and asking good questions.

Navigating Conflict

As a leader, you help set the tone in your organization for how conflict is dealt with. There are several choices you can make to ensure that conflict stays healthy and moves toward stronger relationships:

Accept it and remind yourself that conflict is normal. Don't waste your energy overanalyzing and wondering why you have conflict. Don't let it sink you into a tailspin of self-doubt. Don't moan and groan about it. People hold to different opinions and become angry at times. It's going to be uncomfortable. This is true in our closest relationships as well as our work relationships. Expect conflict but guide it toward shared goals and strengthening relationships.

Choose the best time and place to address it. While there's not always a right time and place, there's usually a *better* time and place to deal with conflict. Although sometimes you have to give a few hours for everyone's emotions to settle, it's not wise to let conflict simmer. It should be dealt with in a timely fashion. Too often leaders ignore conflict, hoping it will all go away. The problem is that it doesn't. Instead, take initiative and face it. Find the best time and the best place that will encourage honest dialogue. The right setting might vary. At times you might choose a conference room or an office. Other times you might choose a coffee shop or a park. Think through the transformation you want to see happen and then take the initiative to get the ball rolling.

Set the ground rules. There are ground rules for a good rumble. It never hurts to reiterate them. Here are the ten commandments on conflict transformation from the wisest man who ever lived:

1. No finger pointing, eye rolling, or name calling. "It's a sin to belittle one's neighbor" (Proverbs 14:21 NLT).

2. No snarky remarks or profanity. "Watch your tongue and keep your mouth shut, and you will stay out of trouble" (Proverbs 21:23 NLT).

3. No exaggerating using phrases like "You always" or "You never." "Telling lies about others is as harmful as hitting them with an ax" (Proverbs 25:18 NLT).

4. No sidebar conversations. "A gossip goes around telling secrets, so don't hang around with chatterers" (Proverbs 20:19 NLT).

5. No filibustering. "Too much talk leads to sin. Be sensible and keep your mouth shut" (Proverbs 10:19 NLT).

6. No jumping to conclusions. "Spouting off before listening to the facts is both shameful and foolish" (Proverbs 18:13 NLT).

7. No assuming the worst. "If you search for good, you will find favor; but if you search for evil, it will find you!" (Proverbs 11:27 NLT).

8. No blaming. "If you roll a boulder down on others, it will crush you instead" (Proverbs 26:27 NLT).

9. No decisions till everyone's heard. "The first to speak in a court sounds right—until the cross-examination begins" (Proverbs 18:17 NLT).

10. No butting in where you don't belong. "Interfering in someone else's argument is as foolish as yanking on a dog's ear" (Proverbs 26:17 NLT).

Manage the story you tell yourself. All of us spin stories in our heads. Have you noticed? Think about a recent conflict. Then consider the story you told yourself. Maybe you told yourself, "He's not giving me the respect I deserve," "To my face they comply but behind my back they are insubordinate," or, "They are blaming me for the financial disaster!" We all spin stories. The key is to only tell yourself the truth. Don't imagine what others are thinking if you don't know. Learn to manage the stories in your head, and your leadership in conflict will be much more effective.

Confront when necessary. It can be tempting to avoid confrontations, hoping problems will simply go away. That's never a good idea because problems don't usually just disappear. Take initiative. A confrontation is simply a face-to-face meeting to resolve a problem. At times you may have to set up a confrontation with a leader who is higher ranking than you in the company. By taking initiative, you'll earn respect. This was the case for our friend Brad.

Brad is a general contractor working on the East Coast. After working as a project manager for several years at a well-known company, he was highly respected and sought after. While running a large project in the heart of Boston, he ran into some issues and profit margins began to dip. When word reached his superior that the project was struggling, his supervisor blew up, using demeaning and belittling language. Brad felt like a complete failure. Other project managers had experienced the same harsh rebukes from the supervisor. The more the men were harassed, the more the

Keys for an effective confrontation:

1. Plan a time and place to meet (don't spontaneously confront someone).
2. Rehearse talking points.
3. Gain a sense of calm before you start.
4. Begin with a positive statement about your intent.
5. Use "I" statements.
6. Describe the effect of the problem.
7. Invite the other person to suggest solutions—and then listen attentively.
8. Stay curious.
9. Restate your commitment to the relationship.
10. Be open to compromise.

jobs struggled. After wrestling for a few weeks over what to do, Brad decided he needed to have a confrontation with his supervisor. He made several pages of notes and decided in advance that this conversation (on his end) was going to be very calm and unemotional.

Brad began the confrontation by describing how the previous meeting made him feel attacked and belittled. He explained that it was not the content of the material covered, but the way it was delivered. He took a posture of curiosity and tried to genuinely understand where his boss was coming from and stated he was receptive to ongoing instructions from the supervisor moving forward. He stayed completely unemotional the whole time.

After listening, Brad's supervisor ended the conversation by saying, "Thank you so much for pointing this out to me. I don't always realize how I come across." Both felt heard and were able to continue working together with new respect for each other.

Stay curious and ask questions. The next time you're pulled into a conflict, pause before you say anything and remind yourself to stay calm and curious. Ask thoughtful, open-ended questions. By asking good questions you demonstrate receptiveness, set a conciliatory tone, and display a genuine interest in dialogue. Our daughter Stefanie recently attended a conference called Faith Walking, where the participants were encouraged to analyze their faith journey in light of the false narratives they had believed along the way. In one of the sessions, a man stood to his feet, clearly agitated, and in an attacking tone confronted the facilitator. Stef was inspired as she watched the facilitator handle and diffuse the conflict by staying curious and asking great questions. We'll let Stefanie describe what happened.

> At the beginning of the day, two of the leaders opened the floor for people to share and receive coaching. A man who appeared obviously nervous began to share. He opened by saying he was hesitant because what he was about to say wouldn't be well-received. At that point, his "sharing" became attacking.
>
> The man used profanity and said that the entire conference was a farce. "We are basically all here to learn how to be adults, which we should all already know how to be."

He then went on to accuse the participants of being the reason he can't bring his nonbelieving friends to church.

I immediately turned to look at the facilitator on the stage. I was expecting him to laugh nervously, suggest they talk privately later, and somehow take the mic away from this very agitated man. Instead, he sat down on the stage. He turned his body to the man, who at this point was quite upset.

The facilitator waited until the man paused, and then he calmly spoke. "Okay, so what I'm hearing you say is that everyone in this room, yourself included, is here to learn how to be an adult. That is super embarrassing to you and is the reason why you don't bring your friends to church. Is that right?"

Immediately, there was a change in the man who was attacking. His entire posture shifted. He said, "No, no, that's not what I'm saying."

The facilitator, still calm and still sitting, said, "Oh, good. So then I guess my question for you is, What is *your* next step? Where do *you* go next, because you can only take responsibility for you, right?"

As an observer, here's what struck me about the entire interaction. First, the facilitator's entire body language invited this man to tell him more. He wasn't trying frantically to get him to stop talking. He didn't appear to be at all threatened by the harsh words. Second, the facilitator didn't try to argue with the man. He asked questions and remained curious. He didn't tell him he was wrong, try to prove his point, or tell him that he needed to calm down.

He allowed him to vent and didn't shame him. Third, the facilitator gently helped the man to shift his focus from accusing everyone else in the room to self-reflection. The man ended up staying for the entire conference and actually shared later that he loved it.

When you remain calm, stay curious, and ask great questions, conflict can be transformational.

Here are a few great questions you can ask:

- From your viewpoint, what triggered this conflict?
- What about this situation do you find most troubling?
- Can you help me understand why you feel this is so important?
- What are you most afraid of or concerned about?
- What would you like to see change?
- Can you tell me more?

Focus on understanding. When you're listening, concentrate on understanding rather than on what you're going to say next. This is not the time for advice, opinions, solutions, or answers. This is the time to seek to understand. Focus your listening on the way you would want to be heard rather than on proving your point.

Paraphrase what you think you heard. "I think I heard you say X. Is this right?" This is exactly what the facilitator of the conference did when the participant became attacking.

By repeating the thoughts of others in your own words, you show them that you are paying attention to what they're saying and are genuinely interested in their thoughts. You also allow them to clarify what they meant and create a less defensive atmosphere. Ultimately, you minimize the chances of misunderstanding.

Validate concerns. Empathy is the capacity to see the world through the lens of another. We honor others when we validate their feelings. It's only when divergent sentiments are respected and valued that we get a full picture. You offer empathy with statements like, "I can see why you'd feel overlooked," or, "It makes sense to me that you're angry," or, "I can see you really feel passionately about this issue." Each of those statements seeks to validate what the other person is feeling. One of the greatest human needs is to feel understood. Once a person feels understood, they will often calm down enough to hear other opinions.

Look for common ground, no matter how small. See where you can find agreement on concerns or changes that can be made. A great question to ask is, "Can we all agree on X?" Be aware of the silent team members. Total silence may be a sign of passive resistance. Take the time to draw quiet participants out by asking them, "What are your thoughts on this issue?" Pursue agreement where there's common ground and work on compromise where there's disagreement.

Determine next steps. A good question to ask is, "Where do we go from here?" or, "What might be the next step?" Bring as many alternatives to the table as possible. Invite the group to collectively decide on the next step. Be sure that all parties have bought in.

Circle back. It's always a good idea to schedule a follow-up meeting just to be sure that the issue is being resolved. Clean it up and clear it out. Hanging on to grudges or clinging to hurts is nothing but a bust. Forgive and let it go.

Above all . . . stay calm. Conflict is anxiety producing. Anxiety impairs your ability to think clearly and listen attentively to others. Breathe deep. Be cool. Keep your emotions grounded. Get a grip. Keep it together. Speak slowly. Be the voice of reason. Don't lose control, pull rank, or say something stupid that you'll regret and need to fix later. As the wise man said, "A gentle answer deflects anger, but harsh words make tempers flare" (Proverbs 15:1 NLT).

A mentor once counseled me (Steve) with these words: "Speak slow, low, last, and without flinching." At the time, I was paddling through the roughest white water of my life. His words served me well.

Conflict is never easy, but it's an amazing opportunity to orchestrate stronger team unity. While it requires courage, patience, humility, and respect, if you navigate conflict well and direct people toward transformation, you'll earn respect rather than ruining your credibility.

QUESTIONS TO ASK YOUR TEAM

1. Have you spoken directly to the other people involved?

2. When did this conflict begin?

3. Is there something I'm missing?

4. Are you willing to share with me how this conflict has impacted you?

5. Do you feel heard/understood?

6. Help me understand your perspective.

7. What about this conflict feels most urgent to you?

8. Where would you like to see this go?

9. What steps do you feel need to be taken in order to compromise?

10. If compromise is not an option, what steps can be taken to make sure the needs of both parties are met?

QUESTIONS FOR SELF-LEADERSHIP

1. What messages did you receive about conflict during your growing-up years? How have those messages impacted your leadership?

2. What triggers defensiveness in you during conflict?

3. If you could change one thing about how you communicate during a conflict, what would it be?

4. How much of your energy is being used up worrying about what others think?

5. What are you willing to compromise on?

6. From your perspective, what is nonnegotiable in this conflict?

7. Do you need to forgive and move on, or take further action?

8

Look for Truth in Criticism

Don't be distracted by criticism. Remember, the
only taste of success some people have is when
they take a bite out of you.

—Zig Ziglar

Key: The leader who listens to
criticism without becoming
defensive earns credibility.

Criticism is hard. Both Steve and I (Becky) have sensitive
spirits and have needed to grow in our ability to handle
criticism without becoming defensive.

As a kid, the thing I heard the most was, "Stop crying. You're too sensitive." That message reverberated in my head for years into my adulthood. Any time criticism came my way, that message repeated itself in my subconscious. I was sure I could never be a leader because of my sensitive spirit. In the face of criticism, I crumbled. At other times, as I mentioned in *How to Listen So People Will Talk*, "I may have come on too strong" in an effort to defend myself.[1]

I remember one time in the beginning of my writing ministry, I received an angry email from a reader who disagreed with my theology. Her words were harsh and felt like bullets. For days I obsessed and couldn't sleep. I finally had to ask myself, "Why can't I let this go? I don't even know this woman." And then, "What can I learn from this?"

God in His mercy graciously met me and showed me how important it was to me to have others like me. He began to show me that the more public my life became and the more influence He allowed me to have, the more criticism was going to come my way. Gradually, I learned that criticism could be my friend if I was able to glean nuggets of truth from it and use it as a catalyst for growth.

I (Steve) also had to grow in my ability to handle criticism. Many who know us well joke that I married Becky because she was a cheerleader, and I needed constant affirmation in my life. There's probably some truth to that. Growing up in a boarding school, I didn't receive a lot of affirmation, so I came to adulthood craving positive feedback. Consequently, criticism felt very hard for me. As soon as I stepped into leadership, I entered the arena where criticism came from every angle.

On my first Sunday as a young pastor, I was approached by an elderly lady who informed me that God had brought me to the church so that she could help me grow. Over the next few months, she mentored me in ways she'd never imagined!

Ray Anne had a reputation. Every pastor within a fifty-mile radius knew her as "Ray Anne the Battering Ram." She had rightfully earned the title. For decades, Ray Anne had made the rounds from church to church, straightening out one pastor after another. Ray Anne was the most cranky and critical person I had ever encountered. She thought she knew the Bible better than anyone else. Her piercing blue eyes and frowning scowl could put the fear of God into the most hardened Philistine.

For reasons unknown to me or anyone else in leadership, Ray Anne had somehow been appointed as the director of guest services in our church. Every Sunday morning she'd stand in the back of the sanctuary on the lookout for newcomers. As long as our guests sported the King James Version of the Bible and were wearing appropriate Sunday dress, Ray Anne would warmly welcome them into the fellowship. Men who carried the wrong Bible version and women who dressed "too fashionably" to stand before the Almighty were quickly apprised of their indiscretions. Few of these visitors returned for a second visit. Ray Anne clearly lacked any kind of seeker sensitivity. She scared people. She terrorized me.

On Sunday mornings when our eighty-six-year-old organist finished her prelude, the Battering Ram would march up the center aisle and take her position on the front pew. Next to her was nestled her dearest companion in life: a prehistoric reel-to-reel tape recorder. As I took my position behind the mahogany monstrosity to deliver the morning message, Ray Anne would dramatically reach over and push Record. The first time it happened, I was immediately inspired with the dreamy notion that Ray Anne was setting me up for a vast and powerful media ministry. I was deluded. On Sunday afternoons, Ray Anne would carefully review the tapes to make sure that the pastor didn't use a swear word or say something heretical. On Monday mornings, I could always count on Ray Anne to rate the previous day's sermon. My ratings were never very high. Most of the time, her criticisms were wildly unhelpful, but every now and then, the Battering Ram could come up with a real gem.

As Winston Churchill once observed, "The greatest lesson in life is to know that even fools are right sometimes." At times the most insightful wisdom can come from the most unlikely source.

As I continued growing into larger and more influential leadership positions, the criticisms didn't stop. They kept coming, at times from all different directions. I once had an administrative assistant who previewed my email. In an attempt to shield me from having to hear and respond to hurtful comments, she would secretly delete offending messages without telling me about them. While I appreciated her thoughtfulness,

I needed to hear what people were thinking. Rather than withdrawing or becoming defensive, I had to grow.

Leaders get criticized. I learned not to take criticism too personally or to respond too defensively. I learned to look for the good and toss out the bad. Most of all, I learned that I needed to listen to criticism in order to grow and become a wise and effective leader.

Invite Criticism?

How you handle criticism will set the tone for your organization and earn the respect or disrespect of your team. If you courageously invite criticism and gracefully listen to it, you will earn loyalty and trust. If you react with defensiveness or withdrawal, you'll lose your credibility. As Proverbs 13:18 states, "If you ignore criticism, you will end up in poverty and disgrace; if you accept correction, you will be honored."

Solomon said, "If you listen to constructive criticism you will be at home among the wise" (Proverbs 15:31). He also said, "Fools think their own way is right, but *the wise listen to others*" (Proverbs 12:15 NLT, emphasis added).

Learning to listen to criticism, even when it's unwarranted and unwanted, is an important leadership skill. As leaders, most of us would agree that "in the end, people appreciate honest criticism far more than flattery" (Proverbs 28:23).

So how do you create an environment where constructive criticism is welcomed and your staff feels safe delivering it?

Ten Principles for Inviting Constructive Criticism

Ask for it. I regularly ask my senior leadership questions like, "What do you think? Is there anything I could or should have said or done differently? How did this come across to you?" I want to know what they are thinking. I value their feedback. Persistently asking questions like these makes my staff feel valued, respected, and appreciated. It makes me a better leader. "To one who listens, valid criticism is like a gold earring" (Proverbs 25:12). It takes courage and vulnerability to ask for critical feedback. The famous American writer Joseph Campbell once noted that the cave you are afraid to enter is the one that holds the treasure you are looking for. If you want to be a better leader, you need to enter the cave; you need to be courageous and unguarded. It never ceases to amaze me how many leaders struggle with being vulnerable. Many of us seem to have the idea that opening up our hearts is a sign of weakness. In reality, it's a sign of great strength. The more you solicit feedback from others, the easier it is to receive.

Slow down and don't react. When being criticized, it's tempting to dive in and change the course of the conversation. Stop. Try not to react. Even for a few seconds, just pause. Interrupting is never helpful. Defending yourself is counterproductive. Blame-shifting and excuse-making will get you nowhere. Stop. Get a grip. Breathe deep. Ask the other person to tell you more. Proverbs 18:13 reminds us that "spouting off before listening to the facts is both shameful and foolish."

A wise pastor friend once told me a story. Long ago, there was a peasant who owned a donkey that was a big disappointment to him. He constantly berated the donkey, calling it names and harassing it with insults. For many months and years, the donkey patiently put up with the insults. Meanwhile, the owner of the beast would go around town telling everyone that his donkey was stupid and lazy. Everyone in town knew that the donkey was just being a donkey. As far as donkeys go, he was a fine donkey. The villagers advised the donkey's owner that he should be kind and gentle, but he was not receptive to their advice. One day when the man came into town with his donkey, the beast was loaded down with a heavy pack of grain. Weary and tired, the donkey lay down for a rest. The owner was furious. In front of everyone in the village, he rained down insults on the donkey and kicked and prodded the poor animal. Finally, the donkey had had enough. Years of resentment had built up. In one final burst of energy, the donkey rose to his feet and suddenly kicked his owner. The donkey's owner yelled out in pain. "See, I told you he was nothing but an ass!" You don't want to be an ass. Don't rush to speak. Don't rush to vindicate yourself. Rein in your impulsiveness. Slow down.

Assume positive intent. Often people mistake criticism for personal attack. Why is it that we tend to think the worst of people who criticize us? We need to manage the stories that we create in our heads. Most people are slow to criticize. If they're willing to risk the relationship with you, they probably have good intentions. Give them the benefit of the doubt.

Focus on the facts. When you focus on your feelings, criticism cuts deeper, feels worse, and lasts longer. Neurologists know that the more primitive part of our brains (the stem) rules our basic human drives (like fight, flight, food, and sex). If this area is highly activated, other more developed parts of our brains recede into the background. Simply put, when our brain stems are highly activated, our feelings become stronger than our thoughts. Focusing on your feelings when confronted with criticism stimulates the exact part of your brain that prevents you from your best thinking. So when listening to criticism, focus on the facts, not your feelings. If need be, pretend in the moment that the criticism is about someone else. When you're in the fight-or-flight mode, you're far less likely to gain any lasting value from the criticism.

Say thanks (but only if you mean it). It might seem trite to say, but well-intentioned constructive feedback is a gift. Journalist Courtney Shea wrote that the best advice she has ever received on criticism came from a former defense attorney who said, "Make eye contact and listen with your mouth shut. If you must open your mouth, it should say 'thank you.'"[2] Expressing appreciation doesn't have to mean that you agree with everything that's being said. However, it does show that you appreciate the effort and commitment of your colleague to share his or her thoughts. For most people, it's difficult to give critical feedback to another person. Appreciate it!

Drill down. Ask for specific examples. Ask for clarification. Stay curious. Stay connected. Don't check out. Don't hurry the process to minimize the pain. There's a mantra we teach our staff: "Tell me more." Solomon once observed, "Though good advice lies deep within the heart, a person with understanding will draw it out" (Proverbs 20:5 NLT). Stephen Covey's fifth habit of highly effective people is this: "Seek first to understand, then to be understood."[3] Covey correctly observes, "Most people do not listen with the intent to understand; they listen with the intent to reply."[4] How true is that! As the person shares their feedback with you, listen closely. Allow them to finish their thoughts without interrupting. Focus on what they are saying.

Own what you can. Everyone makes mistakes. Everyone has blind spots. So do you. Rather than viewing criticism as a personal attack on your worth and validity, view it as a resource for making you a better, more competent leader. If there's any validity to the criticism, own up to it. Admitting that you've made a mistake isn't a sign of weakness. It's a sign of strength. It takes courage and maturity to admit where you've been wrong. When admitting failure or wrongdoing, be specific. Generalized and vague apologies aren't sincere. It's not an authentic apology to say, "I'm sorry if I offended you." It's not genuine to say, "I'm sorry if you took what I said the wrong way." Wow . . . people can say the dumbest things when "apologizing"! When our children were little, we taught them to say to one another, "I was wrong when I did (specific wrongdoing). Will you forgive me?" It takes a strong leader to say those words. You can do it.

Consider the source. Everyone needs to be listened to. Everyone deserves a voice. But some voices should hold more weight to you than others. I don't lose sleep over toxic people. I've met many of them. They used to bother me a lot. Not anymore. Oftentimes they are dealing with issues that go way beyond their concerns with you. I don't feel the need to please everybody or have everyone agree with me. Don't fret the toxics. Ecclesiastes 7:21–22 says, "Do not pay attention to every word people say, or you may hear your servant cursing you—for you know in your heart that many times you yourself have cursed others."

Ask for time to follow up. Sometimes you need space to reflect and process what you've heard. It's okay to say, "Let me think about what you've said and get back to you with my thoughts." Just be sure that you actually act on what you've promised. If you ask for feedback but don't act on the input, your team will stop giving you what you need to hear. It's important to take action, and it's important to let your team know how you acted and how it was received. Don't promise and fail to deliver.

Move on. Yes. Move on. You can choose to take offense and live in a state of bitterness. It's your choice. But if you do, it's your loss. The author of Hebrews said this: "Look after each other so that none of you fails to receive the grace of God. Watch out that no poisonous *root of bitterness* grows up to trouble you, corrupting many" (Hebrews 12:15 NLT, emphasis added).

Criticism isn't easy to hear, but we'd all prefer to have someone criticize us to our faces than dish it out behind our backs.

Leadership Takes Courage

It takes courage to listen and respond graciously. Winston Churchill, who was probably criticized by more people than anyone else in his generation, said this: "Courage is what it takes to stand up and speak; courage is what it takes to sit down and listen."

Do you have the courage to sit down and listen? Have you created a safe environment for your staff to provide feedback and input? How would your staff answer that question?

When you walk away from a difficult feedback session and can honestly say, "I stayed connected, courageous, authentic, and curious," then it's a win. Pat yourself on the back. Remember the words of Theodore Roosevelt:

> It is not the critic who counts; not the man who points out how the strong man stumbles, or where the doer of deeds could have done them better. The credit belongs to the man who is actually in the arena, whose face is marred by dust and sweat and blood; who strives valiantly; who errs, who comes short again and again, because there is no effort without error and shortcoming; but who does actually strive to do the deeds; who knows great enthusiasms, the great devotions; who spends himself in a worthy cause; who at the best knows in the end the triumph of high achievement, and who at the worst, if he fails, at least fails while daring greatly, so that his place shall never be with those cold and timid souls who neither know victory nor defeat.[5]

Learnings

Oh, about Ray Anne the Battering Ram . . . after a few months of giving her the benefit of the doubt and doing my best to get her on my side, I (Steve) finally concluded that it was time to put an end to her toxicity. The mentoring was over.

One day after church I called her to my office with a trusted deacon by my side. Looking her in the eye, I asked the question, "How can I help you become the kind of person that others want to listen to?" Ray Anne was better at dishing out criticism than receiving it. She decided that the Methodists down the street needed more saving than us.

Looking back, we're now thankful for Ray Anne. Why? It was great training for future leadership. The truth is, criticism comes with the territory. Ray Anne had great intentions even though her methods were wrong. Through the years, we've learned that most people have good intentions and are not out to get us. Ray Anne taught us the value of not assuming the worst in others. She also taught us the value of not being driven to keep others happy. Both of us are naturally people pleasers. But people pleasers often end up with stomach ulcers because they simply can't keep everyone happy. At some point, all of us need to come to peace with the fact that not everyone is going to like us, and that's okay. Another lesson we learned was the value of not putting off a confrontation when necessary. As we talked about in the previous chapter, a confrontation is simply a face-to-face meeting to address a problem. While it's wise to take time to pray and think through a plan, you can't put off the inevitable. Eventually, the elephant in the room needs to be brought out in the open.

Criticism will always feel uncomfortable, but it has the potential to shape you into a more influential and effective leader. If you focus your listening ear on finding the truth buried in the criticism, you'll earn credibility, have a more positive outlook, and enjoy more influence.

QUESTIONS TO ASK YOUR TEAM

1. How can you shift your focus to see this criticism as an opportunity for growth?
2. How did you avoid defensiveness?
3. Is there any harm in implementing the idea suggested?
4. What truth can you glean from the critic?
5. Is there a chance you are taking this too personally?
6. How important is this relationship to you?
7. What will be the result if you withdraw from the critic? How will that impact your job performance?
8. How did the conversation end?
9. How will you circle back to be sure your co-worker feels heard?
10. Did you document the conversation? (When it comes to criticism, it's always good to keep a

communication log—with dates—so that you remember what the concerns were and what you promised moving forward).

QUESTIONS FOR SELF-LEADERSHIP

1. Is there anything valuable for you in this criticism?
2. What is the primary concern of the person who is criticizing? (People who are hurting often hurt others. Consider how your critic may be hurting.)
3. What action steps do you need to take for personal growth?
4. Where are you in danger of taking this too personally?
5. How do you move forward to keep the relationship intact and not distance yourself?

9

Listen and Collect Stories

To be good at storytelling leaders must embrace
the art of story listening.

John Maeda

> **Key:** Listen to collect stories.

When we were raising our kids, Steve wanted to give them a heart for the world and a sense of adventure. Most nights before bed, Steve would tell the kids stories. Having grown up in Africa, he had plenty! He told them about his experiences with cobras and vipers. He told them about how he'd been chased by elephants, how he'd preached to baboons, and what it was like to have a monkey as his best friend.

Not all of his stories were about animals. Some of his stories were about poor choices he made and important lessons he learned along the way. For example, Steve and his rowdy junior high friends pretended to pull ropes across the dark roads in Africa in the middle of the night. Truckers would stop, afraid they were going to get robbed. Then the boys would set off firecrackers to spook the truck drivers and run. (Steve's never really been a rule follower.) Unfortunately, one night their tricks turned frightening. The truckers were furious and chased Steve and his friends for two hours. Fortunately, no one got hurt, but Steve describes being terrified and learning the danger of those types of shenanigans.

Steve redeemed his stories of wild junior high antics with stories of his parents' and grandparents' service as missionaries in Africa. Their stories of answered prayer and powerful miracles deeply impacted our kids. Rather than lecturing our kids about spending time in prayer, Steve chose stories that would inspire them in their own prayer journeys.

Steve's tales, affectionately called "Papa's stories," have now been passed down to our grandkids. They are starting to ask, "Papa, when can I go to Africa with you?" His stories are building the next generation of Jesus followers who are excited about the adventure of serving God anywhere.

Donald Miller, *New York Times* bestselling author of *Building a Story Brand*, writes, "Story is the greatest weapon we have to combat noise, because it organizes information in such a way that people are compelled to listen."[1] Stories are memorable. If used well, they have the potential to grow our business and expand our influence.

Storytelling Was God's Idea

Rooted in ancient history, storytelling was God's idea. God knew that if a thought or concept was going to take root in a person's mind, it was best communicated through story. He asked the Israelites to tell the stories of His miracles to their children and to pass them down from generation to generation (Deuteronomy 6:6–7). Many of the Jewish holidays and festivals were celebrations of the great stories of how God had worked miracles on Israel's behalf. Years later, when Jesus walked on earth, His primary teaching method was storytelling. When He wanted us to understand the concept of grace, He told the story of the prodigal son (Luke 15:11–32). When He wanted us to understand the power of love, He told the story of the good Samaritan (Luke 10:25–37). And when He talked about the kingdom, He told the story of the mustard seed (Matthew 13:31–32). Why? Because stories stick!

Companies, corporations, and churches are all adopting God's idea about storytelling. According to *Forbes* magazine, storytelling is the new imperative for businesses.[2] The stories of your company are the greatest tool you have for building brand evangelists. If you want others to believe in your product, tell a story that illustrates how that product will change their lives—and bingo! People will buy. Likewise, if you want others to support your nonprofit, tell a story that describes the impact of your vision.

Often as leaders our primary concern is to craft a compelling message. But if you want a good tag line, first you have to listen. If you want to tell the story of a product that will change the world, first you must learn the art of story *listening*.

The Wisdom of Story Listening

Wise leaders learn to listen to the stories of their employees and clients. They welcome stories about the successes and failures within their company. These stories, when collected, are "like an earring of gold or an ornament of fine gold" (Proverbs 25:12). In other words, great stories are worth their weight in gold.

What's the story of your organization? Stories help humanize an idea, and people would far rather invest in something human than just an idea or concept. The stories of transformation from your company have the potential to shape the trajectory of the future of your organization. So how do you start listening for stories, and how do you know which stories are important? Here are a few ideas:

Listen for the problem within the story of your client. "Customers don't generally care about your story; they care about their own."[3] This means that your brand means squat unless it's meeting the client's need. Too many companies are answering questions that no one is asking. Instead, start with your client—and intentionally listen. Figure out what his problem is and then come up with a solution.

Genevieve Piturro did this. She was volunteering at a shelter for homeless children in New York City and decided to bring twelve pairs of pajamas to help the kids get ready for bed. When she arrived, she realized that some children at the shelter didn't even know what pajamas were because they had always just slept in their clothes. Genevieve was so moved that in 2001 she founded The Pajama Program, which is an organization that works to give new pajamas and books to children in shelters, group homes, and other places where the need is great. As a result, children's lives were changed because Genevieve listened, not only with her ears but with her heart, to the clients in the homeless shelters. Her entire nonprofit is built around solving that one problem. Children need pajamas, and her company provides them. Because of The Pajama Program, children can crawl into bed comfortably and feel at home even in a homeless shelter.

Messaging is everything, but before you craft a great tag line, you must listen to figure out what dilemma your client is facing. How does your product offer a solution? How will your product transform his or her life and make it better?

Listen to build brand evangelists. Great stories of success engage the heart and motivate team members to keep going. According to *Forbes* magazine, "Emotional engagement is proving to be more and more critical to achieving winning results and effective storytelling is at the heart of this movement."[4]

If you want to build an army of brand evangelists, you need to listen to gather testimonials of transformation. Dave Ramsey, the founder of Financial Peace University, has done this with his radio show.

The Dave Ramsey radio show hosts a testimonial time that's known as "The Debt-Free Scream." Dave interviews folks on his show and listens as the guests explain the amount of debt they have paid off. Each story marks a life that's been changed by Dave Ramsey's Financial Peace University. After each story is told, the guest is encouraged to scream their debt-free scream. Confetti falls in the studio as the audience listens to the celebratory scream. Others are inspired and believe they can do it too! It is a brilliant marketing plan on Dave Ramsey's part. By listening well to stories of success, he has built a massive army of brand evangelists. It gives him credibility that his product works. If used well, stories will become the backbone of your marketing strategy.

I (Becky) have always felt a bit intimidated by marketing. When I was getting ready to release *How to Listen So People Will Talk*, I had the opportunity to talk through my insecurities in the marketing realm with Chad Cannon, who is the head of marketing for Michael Hyatt's company. Michael founded Platform University as well as other companies. He is a master at helping leaders build their platforms. In our conversation, Chad took some of the fear and mystery out of marketing for me. He helped me understand that marketing is really about story listening and storytelling. If you intentionally listen for stories of transformation and tell those stories to others, people are automatically motivated. As I began telling the stories of how relationships were being changed as people worked on their listening skills, people wanted to buy the book. They realized that some of their own relationships were suffering because they didn't know how to listen. They wanted a product that would transform their relationships. *How to Listen So People Will Talk* offered that promise.

Listen to stories of failure. Our friend Tom was the executive pastor of a large church. Every week in his staff meeting he asked, "Who failed well this week?" Each story of failure was celebrated as a learning tool. By encouraging people to share their stories of failure, Tom removed the shame element.

The founder of the successful company Spanx, Sara Blakely learned early that every failure could be transformed into success. During her growing-up years, every Friday night at the dinner table, her father would ask her and her brother, "What did you fail at this week?"[5] That question set the stage for Sara to realize later in life that even failures can lead to greater success. By listening to Sara and her brother's stories of failure, their dad set the stage for them to be successful in leadership later.

Failure can be one of the greatest life lessons. Reflecting on where we've failed allows us to develop a deeper understanding of where we're at as a business or nonprofit and where we need to improve. Our failures reveal our blind spots and help us to delve more deeply into where we can improve.

Harvard business school professor Rob Kaplan teaches his students to perfect both their success stories and their failure stories. These stories help future leaders understand themselves better. They get a truer picture of their personal quirks, insecurities, and blind spots. After the young leaders become aware of these, they are more prepared to move into leadership in the future.[6]

The same principle holds true for organizations as a whole. When the leader is not fearful of stories of failure, the entire organization becomes more aware of their blind spots, places where they've dropped the ball, or how they're perceived by those outside the company. Stories of failure help your team understand that failure isn't the end of the world; it's often the stepping-stone toward greater success.

How to Find the Stories That Define Your Company

You might be thinking, *Well, sure, it's great to listen and collect stories, but how do I get started?* Great question! Here are a few ideas for you:

Be intentional about asking. That seems pretty obvious, but at times we don't hear stories because we're not asking for them. Make it a practice to ask regularly, perhaps at your weekly staff meetings, for stories of both success and failure. Generally, people will be more willing to tell the stories of success, but if people feel safe and become accustomed to being asked, they will grow more comfortable sharing stories of failure as well.

Create a storyboard in an open gathering place of your office. Encourage team members to post stories that will encourage others. In the mobilization department at Reach Beyond, we recently created a storyboard for Thanksgiving. People posted their stories of giving thanks. Those stories were an encouragement to everyone who took the time to stop and read them. You could use the same idea for stories whenever you're rolling out a new product. Keep a storyboard to collect the stories of those whose lives have been changed by your product.

Keep a journal and fill it with stories. Writing stories in a journal or on your phone will keep the details fresh in your mind. As we travel all over the world, we hear amazing stories, but we have discovered we can't keep all the details straight without recording them. Writing down the key points of the story helps a lot!

Celebrate stories regularly. We're firm believers in celebrating and having a great party from time to time. Celebrations encourage those on your team that the solution or service you're offering works! Stories and celebrations seem to go hand and hand.

The Shandy Clinic provides exceptional therapy for exceptional children. They serve the whole child, offering occupational therapy, physical therapy, speech therapy, and applied behavioral analysis all under one roof.

Stories are a huge part of how the Shandy Clinic keeps their employees on track with vision and how they integrate new team members. I asked Amy Shandy to describe how they use stories to keep their team motivated and how they celebrate.

> We use our stories of success (and failures actually, too) every month in our Newcomers Celebration (new employee orientation), in our Oldcomers Celebration (refresher orientation for those who have worked for us awhile but started before we implemented Newcomers Celebration), and at our company Christmas party, where we love on and celebrate our amazing team. The history and stories of the company help weave our employees into the tapestry of the company. The stories give them a solid foundation of who we are, where we've come from, why we do what we do, and how we do it; it's a launch pad for them to jump from and start weaving their own experiences into the company tapestry. It's really been a beautiful thing to watch strangers come in, choose to be a part of what we're doing, and then carry that on to help children. We've watched these stories grow our company beyond what we imagined.

A thriving communications company called BombBomb celebrates stories of team members with what's called the "Awesome Office." Our friend Darin Dawson is one of the founders of BombBomb and described the Awesome Office for us:

> The Awesome Office is one of three corner offices. It's equipped with a mini-fridge, sofa, desk, soundbar, and other nice adds. This is a major upgrade for the large portion

of employees who work at smaller desks in an open office environment. It brings our core values off the website and down off the wall and makes them real. It's a celebration of relationships, fun, humility, flexibility, and service—a chance to publicly and personally recognize employee and customer behavior that positively reinforces our values. It also generates stories that can be shared and retold; it helps create myth, history, and legacy.

Here's how it works: Every other week, a nomination period opens up. Any team member can nominate another person for a core value they've demonstrated with a video or short write-up. The current office holder who's ending her or his two-week stay in the office chooses from the nominations. At the all-team lunch on Friday, every nomination is read or played in front of everyone, and the winner is announced. Of course, a short speech is demanded by the crowd. Sometimes it's a simple, short thank-you. Other times it's a significant statement. Some have even generated standing ovations.

Both the Shandy Clinic and BombBomb know how to celebrate the stories of success from their companies.

Let's Come Back to Jesus

We realize that story listening could sound completely like a marketing strategy. While it is an effective marketing strategy, beyond marketing it's a way to help people feel honored and valued.

Earlier in this chapter we said that storytelling was God's idea and that Jesus used stories all the time in His teaching. But Jesus also took the time to listen to the stories of others. When He was in a rush to get to Jairus's house to heal his dying daughter, Jesus stopped and took the time to listen to a woman who had been ostracized by society pour out her whole story (Luke 8:40–56). For someone to pour out his or her whole story takes time. As leaders, it's easy to be in a hurry and wanting to move on to the next thing. What Jesus modeled for us is profound. By listening to the woman's story, Jesus gave her dignity and worth. Isn't that what we want our team members and clients to feel?

Every follower wants to know, "Does my leader care about me?" If they don't feel you care, why should they follow? When you as the leader take time to listen to your team's stories of success and failure, you demonstrate that you care. Like Jesus, you provide the space for people to process their experiences. When you listen to the stories of your team, you provide the fabric of trust for the relationship. You validate that each member of your team is important.

QUESTIONS TO ASK YOUR TEAM

1. What's your story?
2. What drew you to this company?

3. What's the best failure you've experienced this week? What did you learn from that perceived failure?

4. What will you do differently next time?

5. Which client did you meet with this week, and how did his or her story impact you?

6. Whose life have you seen transformed this week?

7. Are we asking the right questions as a company? What questions should we be asking to identify problems our clients are facing?

8. How can we better celebrate stories of success?

9. How can we keep the stories of transformation in front of team members so that they stay motivated?

10. Where do you feel we need to improve our messaging?

QUESTIONS FOR SELF-LEADERSHIP

1. Where do you need to create space in your schedule to intentionally listen to the stories of others?

2. What has been the most compelling story you've heard in the last week? How did you record that story?

3. What is the primary need of your clients, and how does your product meet that need?

4. How do you encourage team members to share stories of perceived failure without creating a sense of

shame? How do you encourage each member of your team to fail forward?

5. Which team member consistently reports stories in your team meetings?

6. How do you personally celebrate the stories of success from your team?

10

Create Sacred Space to Reflect and Listen to God

Discernment requires us to move beyond our reliance on cognition and intellectual hard work to a place of deep listening and response to the Spirit of God within and among us.

—Ruth Haley Barton

Key: Create sacred space to listen to God.

(Steve) have always had a deep respect and admiration for Dr. Bill Bright, founder of Cru (Campus Crusade for Christ). When I was fifteen years old, Dr. Bright came to our town. The arena was packed. After the event, hundreds of people were gathered around him. I just wanted a few minutes with my hero, but there was no way I was going to get anywhere close to him. So I did something that only a brash teen would think of. I found out where he was staying. Late that night, I snuck out of the house and rode my bicycle over to his hotel room. I knocked on the door. There he was. Dr. Bright, standing in his bathrobe. I'll never forget the next half hour that we spent together. Most of it was spent on our knees praying together.

Years later, I met up with Dr. Bright once again. At the time, I was serving on the board of directors of a major mission agency that was considering moving its headquarters to Orlando. Cru had just offered to sell us a piece of property adjacent to their headquarters building. Our board was cautious but open. In preparation for our meeting with Dr. Bright and the board of Cru, our directors spent a couple of hours compiling our list of questions and concerns. When the time came for our meeting with Dr. Bright, we were fully prepared. Our chairman launched into the meeting by saying, "Dr. Bright, we've pulled together our list of questions and concerns about building on Crusade's property. Before we get into sharing our concerns, we'd like to invite you to share your concerns with us." I watched Dr. Bright closely. He smiled broadly and folded his arms. "What concerns? Why would anyone have concerns? This is a God-thing. Let's do it." I will not forget that moment as long as I live. Such faith!

I had one more opportunity to cross paths with Dr. Bright. A year before he died, I wrote him a personal letter asking him one question: "Where did your great faith come from?" My letter was short. He wrote two full pages back, talking about walking in the Spirit and listening to God. Through prolonged and active listening to the Spirit, Dr. Bright had become familiar with the voice of his heavenly Father.

Learning to listen and respond to the voice of the Holy Spirit is one of life's greatest challenges and blessings. Though some criticized Bill Bright for claiming to hear from God, none could argue with the integrity of his life and the impact of his leadership.

Most leaders' lives are packed full of important meetings and urgent tasks. It's tempting to just keep going full tilt on the adrenaline rush of leadership without considering the voice of God. Wisdom, however, teaches a different priority: "Fear of the LORD is the foundation of wisdom. Knowledge of the Holy One results in good judgment" (Proverbs 9:10 NLT). As a leader, while it's important that you listen to people, it is most important that you listen to the voice of the Holy Spirit. We were designed to hear from God and cultivate a relationship with Him. As we pull away to hear from God, He gives wisdom, and if there's anything today's leaders need, it's wisdom!

Face Time with God

Moses was one of the greatest leaders of all times. Often insecure in his leadership and up to his neck with the challenges of leading a difficult group of people, Moses developed the practice of face time with God. He regularly hiked up the mountain to seek the Lord for wisdom. During those intimate times with God, Moses was able to shut out the noise of the world and listen to God's voice. There he reflected on the status of his soul and the condition of his leadership (Exodus 33:11). When Moses felt discouraged, he authentically poured out his heart to God, and God attentively listened. When Moses needed wisdom, he asked, and listened to God's answer. He cultivated an extraordinary friendship with God, the kind of relationship we desire with Him. Out of the depth of his relationship with God, Moses learned to discern the Holy One's voice.

In our lives and yours, there are many voices vying, even screaming, for our attention. We need to follow Moses' example in order to lead with wisdom and clarity. We must create sacred space for face time with God. His voice matters above all others.

The idea of "hearing from God" raises quite a few questions: Does God still speak today? Are people who claim to hear from God simply delusional? If God speaks, how do we as humans hear His voice? What does it look like to orchestrate our lives and leadership around His voice? These are the questions we hope to answer in this chapter.

The Case for Hearing God's Voice

God created us for relationship with himself (Exodus 29:43–46; Isaiah 41:8). How can we have a relationship without conversation? Furthermore, we can't have conversations without listening. Conversations go two ways. In fact, most experts advise following the 80/20 rule: Spend 80 percent of your time listening and only 20 percent of your time talking. Thankfully, God is full of grace, and He doesn't hold us to that standard. It is a great reminder, though, that in our relationship with God, our conversations are to involve not only praying and asking for things but also listening for God to speak.

Throughout the Bible, there are numerous stories of people hearing from God. Abram heard God's voice telling him to leave his family and move to new territory (Genesis 12:2). As we've already mentioned, Moses went up to the mountain to hear God's voice (Exodus 19:3). In the New Testament, while the believers were fasting, praying, and worshiping, the Holy Spirit spoke to them to "set apart Paul and Barnabas" as missionaries (see Acts 13:2). Biblically, divine encounters were the norm.

Jesus instructed us in John 10:27–28 that His sheep hear His voice. It is expected that if you follow Jesus, you will recognize and listen to His voice. A study of church history shows this to be true. The greatest leaders of the faith heard from God: Teresa of Avila, Saint Francis of Assisi, Martin Luther, John Wesley, D. L. Moody, Andrew Murray, Frank Laubach, A.W. Tozer, Henri Nouwen, and Bill Bright to name just a few. Unfortunately, many in the Western world have decided that God doesn't speak today. Many feel God stopped speaking when the Bible was complete. Let's clarify.

The primary way God speaks is through Scripture. He also speaks through the still, small voice of His Spirit, through people, through creation, and any other way He desires. It is important to remember that regardless of the method God uses to speak, His words will never contradict Scripture.

As we have had the privilege of traveling around the world, we've heard extraordinary stories of God speaking. In a part of the world where Christ is not known, a religious leader kept hearing a voice in his head that said, "I am the door." Frustrated and fearful, he went to an exorcist and asked that the voice in his head be removed. Despite the best efforts of the exorcist, the voice only grew louder. One night just before evening prayers, a figure appeared in the doorway of the religious leader's bedroom. He boldly asked the figure to reveal himself. There stood Jesus with an angel on His right and His left. Jesus spoke, "I am the way, the truth, and the life. Now go and tell everyone you know!" The religious leader's life was totally transformed. Today, he continues to risk his life by telling others about his faith in Jesus.

Sometimes God speaks through the miraculous, although many times it's through the quiet whisper of His Spirit while you are reading the Scriptures. As a leader it's important to know how to listen for His voice and how to discern between His voice and your own imagination. This is why we believe a daily time of personal reflection is necessary for wise leadership.

Create Space to Be Attentive to God's Love

When we speak of time for personal reflection, we're not referring to time to reflect on trends in leadership or current ideas on finance; rather, we're talking about creating the space to listen attentively to the voice that calls you "Beloved."

Unfortunately, many leaders don't slow down long enough to practice face time with God. Calendars are full and schedules packed. This is a mistake. We were designed to know God and enjoy being known by Him. In His presence we bring our authentic selves—our insecure, inadequate, driven, neurotic, and narcissistic selves—to receive God's love. Those who don't find that deep-seated security in God's love end up living fractured lives trying to prove their worth. As a result, they are unaware and unable to stay tuned in to their true selves.

In his profound book *Abba's Child*, Brennan Manning describes what happens when leaders lose touch with their true selves and create a pseudo-self. Manning writes, "Imposters draw their identity not only from achievements but from interpersonal relationships. They want to stand well with people of prominence because that enhances a person's resume and sense of self-worth." He continues, "The imposter must be called out of hiding, accepted and embraced."[1] How many times have we witnessed leaders who go off the rails, allowing power to distort their thinking because they have lost touch with their true self?

Only when we realize how deeply we are loved can we echo the words of the psalmist David and pray, "Search me, God, and know my heart; test me and know my anxious thoughts" (Psalm 139:23). There in the sacred space of His presence are healing and grace.

If we're going to listen attentively to God's voice and be able to discern what He is saying, we will need to have some intentional spiritual practices surrounding our face time with God.

Intentional Practices to Open Your Ears to Hear God's Voice

Meditation on the Scriptures. Meditation has been recommended by millions as a technique to manage stress. It's been proven to reduce stress, control anxiety, improve memory and focus, enhance self-awareness, lengthen your attention span, and even make you a kinder person.[2]

Since the Bible is the primary way God speaks, it's the perfect focus for your meditation. Don't just read the Bible like a textbook; read it with intentionality. Slow down. Look upward to think about God's heart as you read; then look inward to consider how His words apply to your life. Reflect on what the passage teaches you about God. Mull it over. Then consider how you might apply that passage to your life.

For example, perhaps you wrestle with anxiety; you might even be a little OCD. As you read Philippians 4:6, "Do not be anxious about anything," you think, *That's not even possible!* But then you read a little further and begin meditating on the words that follow:

In every situation, by prayer and petition, with thanksgiving, present your requests to God. And the peace of God, which transcends all understanding, will guard your hearts and your minds in Christ Jesus. Finally, brothers and sisters, whatever is true, whatever is noble, whatever is right, whatever is pure, whatever is lovely, whatever is admirable—if anything is excellent or praiseworthy—think about such things.

vv. 6–8

As you meditate on what the apostle Paul meant, you realize this could be a plan for how to handle your anxiety. In our experience, the people who are the calmest and most influential leaders are those who have learned to meditate on Scripture.

Silence. We are committed to authenticity, and here's the truth: Silence is hard for both of us. When we sit in silence, a million thoughts barrage our brains. Steve jokes that our thoughts are like a bunch of monkeys swinging randomly from tree to tree. When we get busy and overbooked, it only gets worse.

It's easy to ride the adrenaline rush of busyness, especially when our travel schedule is full. Yet silence is an important part of our brain reigniting. We need to create the space for silence if we're going to listen to our souls and listen to God.

Start with a few minutes per day. Juliet Funt, founder of WhiteSpace at Work, is a self-proclaimed "warrior against reactive busyness." She encourages leaders to look at their calendars and find white space—a space where no appointment is listed—so that they can have time to reflect. I (Becky) watched a brief video where Juliet suggested practicing a few minutes of white space where you turn off technology and simply daydream. Apparently, this practice helps reboot your brain's productivity.[3] We would like to suggest claiming white space to enjoy God's presence and listen attentively for His voice.

Both of us practice face time with God in the early morning. During that time, we read the Scriptures, we worship, we pray, and we give thanks. When we pray, God is an attentive listener (1 Peter 3:12). Just as God listens attentively to us, so we need to offer that same attunement to Him. As author Henri Nouwen explained, it's not about hearing a "hallucinatory voice, but about a voice that can be heard by the ear of faith, the ear of the inner heart."[4]

We also try to take a purposeful pause for silence and reflection midday. Usually this silent break is only a few minutes. The silence refreshes our souls and helps us recalibrate. We are able to reflect on anything new we've learned and what God might be speaking.

Sometimes, I (Becky) close my eyes for fifteen minutes. Or I might take a few minutes to simply gaze at the beauty of the mountains that surround our home. During these moments of silence, I try to be aware of my breathing. I exhale any stressful thoughts or anxiety, and I imagine my lungs being refilled with the Holy Spirit's presence and power. I don't have an agenda during these few minutes other than to enjoy God's presence.

I (Steve) find the wilderness a great place for silence. I will often take a hike, and there in the silence breathe in the beauty of God's creation, and often hear God's Spirit speaking from deep within.

Your addiction to busyness and noise will rob your relationship with God if you allow it to. Charles Stone of StoneWell Ministries writes, "Hurry and noise and incessant busyness are enemies of a healthy spiritual life."[5] What if instead you created white space to listen to God? To get you started, try this:

Read from Scripture and then sit quietly. Reflect on what you read and ask God what He wants you to hear from that passage. While you are silent and still, He might speak through the small whisper of His Spirit. Maybe He'll give you a picture of what to do in a given situation. Maybe He will plant a thought in your mind of how to solve a problem. Don't be discouraged if you don't hear anything right away. He might speak later in the day. He might speak through a friend or in any number of different ways. The key is to provide the space and quiet so that when He does speak, you can hear His voice.

Praise and thanksgiving. Twenty years ago, when I (Becky) had just been diagnosed with breast cancer, my mentor challenged me to spend the first twenty minutes of every day for a week praising God. Quite frankly, I thought it was a bit of a ridiculous challenge. I hardly felt like shouting, "Hallelujah!" But after considering her challenge, I decided I had nothing to lose. I took that challenge and within the first five days, that simple practice of praising God had changed my life. Praise opened my ears to the voice of the Holy Spirit in ways I never dreamed possible.

Together as a couple at dinner, we practice reflecting on our day and writing down our top three blessings of the day. This little practice has brought us joy and peace in the evening as we consider how blessed we are. As we cultivate gratitude, the tenor of our home becomes joy.

In the book of Acts, we read that while the early believers were worshiping, the Holy Spirit spoke to them to set aside Paul and Barnabas for missionary work (Acts 13:2). Often it is during times of worship that we recognize God's voice. As we praise God, we shift our focus from our problems to His almighty power. He brings our spirit into alignment with His, and it becomes easier to hear His voice. When we choose to spend time purposefully praising God, the Holy Spirit opens our ears to His voice.

Five Questions to Ask Yourself When Discerning God's Voice

As you intentionally put these practices into place, you'll begin to hear from God. But you might be thinking, *How do I discern between my own thinking and God's voice?* Great question! When we're trying to discern whether or not we've heard from God, particularly in the area of decision-making, we ask ourselves five questions.

What am I seeing in the Scriptures? Paul wrote to Timothy, "All Scripture is God-breathed and is useful for teaching, rebuking, correcting and training in righteousness" (2 Timothy 3:16). One of the most powerful ways to hear God's voice is in your daily Bible reading. As you read, look for patterns and write them down. Often you will find that God is speaking. For example, when Steve was considering the position of CEO at Reach Beyond, we took several days of prayer and looked for patterns in our Bible reading. Verses we read during that time included Isaiah 43:19, "See, I am doing a new thing!"; Isaiah 45:2, "I will go before you and will level the mountains"; and Isaiah 45:4, "I summon you by name." From those verses and many others, we concluded that God was directing us to say yes to the new position. Our hearts were reassured that God was leading and leveling the path before us. We could trust His love.

What do I sense the Holy Spirit is saying? At times you may feel an inner prompting to share your faith with someone. Other times you may feel God prompting you to give money to the homeless man on the street corner. When you feel that inner prompting, act on it. Chances are it has come to you from the Holy Spirit. When you are worshiping or fasting, pause and consider, *What is the Spirit speaking to me?* Remember, it is about listening with an ear of faith.

What are my mentors or close friends saying? The wise writer of Proverbs tells us that "victory is won through many advisers" (Proverbs 11:14). Often when we have been wrestling with a big decision, we consult those who know us best. Close friends and mentors have agreed to pray with us, seek God's face, and then speak into our decision. Over the years, that guidance has served us well. Life is complicated; when faced with huge decisions, you want to be sure you've heard God correctly. Practice leaning into your community as you seek to hear God's voice. Discernment on a particular issue will often come to a group as each one seeks the Lord's face.

What is the best use of my resources? Each of us has been given resources such as talents, gifts, and abilities. God holds us responsible for how we invest those resources. Jesus once told a story about a man who went on a journey and gave gifts to each of his employees, asking them to invest what he had given. When the master returned, he discovered two of the servants had invested all their gifts and grew those gifts to their greatest potential. One servant, however, buried his and didn't intentionally cultivate or invest those gifts. The master scolded the man who didn't put any effort into nurturing his gifts, and told him he was worthless (Matthew 25:14–27).

When you are trying to discern the voice of God in decision-making, teach yourself to ask this question: "What is the best use of my resources?" God wants all of us to be responsible for any asset He's given, but He holds leaders to an especially high standard in this realm. Not only does He call us to discern the best investment of our personal resources, but our company's resources as well.

What is the way of faith? When God speaks, He usually calls us to take a risk and grow deeper in our faith. In our journey, we cannot remember any time when God spoke to us and told us to play it safe. Perhaps others have had those experiences, but usually for us, God speaks and invites us to take a bold step of faith. Bold faith involves risk. When we're trying to determine if we've heard the voice of God correctly, we often ask, "What is the way of faith?" If it involves faith, we can almost guarantee that God is speaking!

A Final Promise and Prayer

We've come on quite a journey through this book as we've considered learning to listen well in order to lead better. Our journey has included becoming more self-aware, knowing our people, giving the gift of empowerment, discerning unspoken values, inviting others to help shape the vision, engaging conflict constructively, looking for the truth in criticism, collecting stories, and finally, most important, creating sacred space to listen to God. As you put the principles that we've written about into practice, we believe your teams will feel more deeply valued, trust will grow, and your leadership will thrive.

As you learn to listen to God, you will be able to let go of the false self that you have created to make yourself look better as a leader. The more attentive you become to God's voice of love, the more secure and confident you're going to feel.

Learning to listen really is the key to greater influence! As we close this chapter and our journey to learn to listen more attentively, take a moment to pause and pray,

Lord, I want to be your instrument. Help me to become more attentive in my listening both to others and to you so that I may reflect your heart more effectively. I want those around me to feel valued, respected, and honored.

Show me how to grow in my ability to be present to you, and ground me more deeply in your love. As I

think through various aspects of my leadership, teach me to bring to you my most authentic self. "I let go of my desire for affirmation and approval. I let go of my desire for security and success. I let go of my desire for power and control."[6] Help me to listen with your ears so that I may lead with your heart.

QUESTIONS FOR SELF-LEADERSHIP

1. What was your most significant takeaway from this book?
2. What is one practice you can put into place after reading this book?
3. What did you learn about offering empathy to others? What needs to change in order for you to be more empathetic with your team?
4. What is one principle you learned about dealing with conflict and initiating confrontation?
5. What have been your obstacles to spending time with God each day? How can you remove those obstacles so that you can prioritize listening to God?

REFLECTIVE EXERCISE ON LISTENING TO GOD

Read Mark 10:46–52 several times through. It can be helpful to read it out loud. Then sit silently for a few moments.

1. Imagine you are having an encounter with Jesus and He asks you, "What do you want me to do for you?" (Mark 10:51). How would you answer?

   Answer this question with regard to the five different aspects of your life.

   Physical:

   Emotional:

   Relational:

   Vocational:

   Spiritual:

2. Though many rebuked blind Bartimaeus for shouting out, he continued to call out to Jesus, "Have mercy on me!" What does this speak to you personally about persistence in prayer?

3. Jesus says to Bartimaeus, "Your faith has healed you" (Mark 10:52). How does your faith in Christ impact your wholeness? How does it impact your leadership?

4. When Jesus has this encounter with Bartimaeus, He is on the way to Jerusalem to be crucified. What does the crucifixion speak to you personally?

5. What does this passage teach about demonstrating mercy?

6. In the passage immediately before the encounter with Bartimaeus, Jesus gives His mandate on leadership: "Instead, whoever wants to become great among you

must be your servant, and whoever wants to be first must be the slave of all. For even the Son of Man did not come to be served, but to serve, and give his life as a ransom for many" (Mark 10:43–45). Jesus is not saying serve others by leading; rather, He is saying lead others by serving. What does this look like in your leadership? Write down specific steps you can take to serve those you lead.

7. What part does attentive listening play in serving others?

8. What does this passage speak to you about empowering broken people?

9. Read the passage again, out loud, slowly. What do you feel God is saying to you through this story?

10. End your time by writing out a prayer to God summarizing your feelings. At first writing out your prayers might feel weird, but we have discovered that often we can express ourselves more authentically when we write our prayers. So give it a try and see what you think. If you find it helpful, you'll want to continue the practice. If not, find a practice for you that helps you communicate with God.

Acknowledgments

Just as no one leads a company to success single-handedly, no one writes a book on their own. It takes a team.

We'd like to thank . . .

Our Kids and Kids-in-Love . . .

Bethany and Chris Lindgren, thanks for helping us process ideas, and for listening as we wrestled with different concepts to make the book stronger. Thanks for the effort you put into helping us edit. We love your hearts for adoption and those in foster care. What a joy to see you guys step into your calling to help the church connect with those in foster care. We are so proud of you and love you so much!

JJ (Josiah) and Shaina Harling, thanks so much for all the listening you did and the feedback you gave as we wrote this book. JJ, it is such a joy to watch your influence grow in the nonprofit world, and Shainey, your influence at the wound-care clinic. You are both such incredible parents, seeking to empathize and understand your kids. You have a deep understanding of how to listen and lead. We are incredibly proud of you both and love you so much!

Stefanie and Dave Holder, wow, what a joy it's been to watch the two of you step up in leadership both professionally and personally at your church! Your hearts to listen to those who have attended the Alpha course with you, as well as your hearts to listen to those you work with, have been such a joy for us to see. You are amazing parents! We love you both and are so proud of you!

Keri and Zach Denison, what a joy to watch both of you grow in your leadership! Keri, you are an incredible worship leader and mentor to those looking to grow deeper in Christ. Zach, you are an incredible leader and teacher for the navy. Watching your influence grow has been such a joy! You are awesome parents seeking to lead your kids toward Jesus. We are so proud of you both and love you so much!

Our Grandkids . . .
Charlie, Tyler, Joshua, Selah, Zachary, Theo, Noah, Rayna, Cayden, Kinley, Tori, and Melody! Wow—words can't express how awesome each of you is! You are all growing leaders who are going to be world-changers! Mimi and Papa love you all so much and can't wait to see what God continues to do in your lives as you grow up!

Those from the publishing industry . . .

Our incredible agent, Blythe Daniels! Blythe, thank you for not only representing us so well but also for hearing our hearts and understanding our passion for godly leadership! Beyond being our agent, you are an incredible friend!

Jeff Braun, thank you for seeing the potential in this book and for guiding us toward the vision. Thanks for taking the time to get to know us both and to pray on our behalf as we seek to lead.

Ellen Chalifoux, thank you for your masterful editing! We couldn't do this without you!

All the incredible men and women at Bethany House Publishers. We love and appreciate you!

Suzanne Kuhn and all the wonderful team members from Brookstone Creative Group. Thank you for the opportunities you have opened for us and the coaching you have given us in getting our message out! We love you!

Our incredible board members from Reach Beyond! You guys have prayed with us and stood by us as we have led Reach Beyond through some significant changes! We love you and will be forever grateful to you!

The many friends and family members who have prayed for us as we have written! You know who you are and we could never have done this without you!

Notes

Chapter 1 The Missing Ingredient to Greater Influence

1. Rob Bogosian and Christine Casper, "The Leading Cause of Corporate Calamity Is Leaders Who Don't Listen," *Entrepreneur*, May 19, 2015, www.entre preneur.com/article/246376.

2. Gallup, *State of the American Workplace* (Washington, D.C.: Gallup, 2017), 2, www.bcivic.org/wp-content/uploads/2016/08/GALLOP-2017-State-American -Workplace_Report_gen_webfinal_rj.pdf.

3. Dietrich Bonhoeffer, *Life Together* in *Life Together and Prayerbook of the Bible* (Dietrich Bonhoeffer Works, Vol. 5), trans. Daniel W. Bloesch and James H. Burtness (Minneapolis: Fortress, 2005), 98.

Chapter 2 Become Self-Aware, Not Self-Obsessed

1. Tom Rath and Barry Conchie, *Strengths Based Leadership* (New York: Gallup, 2008), 11.

2. Brené Brown, *Daring Greatly* (New York: Avery, 2012), 22.

Chapter 3 Know Your People

1. Kyle Benson, "The Human Heart Was Made to Be Known and Loved," www.kylebenson.net/heart-known.

2. Becky Harling, *How to Listen So People Will Talk* (Minneapolis: Bethany House, 2017), 48.

3. Kim Scott, *Radical Candor* (New York: St. Martin's Press, 2017), 4.

4. Adapted from Harling, *How to Listen So People Will Talk*, 108–112.

5. William A. Gentry, Todd J. Weber, and Golnaz Sadri, *Empathy in the Workplace: A Tool for Effective Leadership* (Center for Creative Leadership, 2016), 2, www.ccl.org/wp-content/uploads/2015/04/EmpathyInTheWorkplace.pdf.

6. Harling, *How to Listen So People Will Talk*, 90.

7. "State of the American Workplace," February 2017, http://news.gallup.com/reports/178514/state-american-workplace.aspx.

8. Ekaterina Walter, "Four Essentials of Strength-Based Leadership," *Forbes*, August 27, 2013, www.forbes.com/sites/ekaterinawalter/2013/08/27/four-essentials-of-strength-based-leadership/#3b49084d64c9.

9. "Affirming Leadership," Discprofiles, October 16, 2018, www.discprofiles.com/blog/2018/10/affirming-leadership.

10. Nancy Beach, "What's So Great about the Enneagram?" August 25, 2014, www.nancylbeach.com/blog/2014/8/25/whats-so-great-about-the-enneagram.

Chapter 4 Give the Gifts of Trust and Empowerment

1. Sujan Patel, "10 Examples of Companies With Fantastic Cultures," *Entrepreneur*, August 6, 2015, https://www.entrepreneur.com/article/249174.

2. "How Successful Leaders Use Empowerment to Build Trust and Excellence," http://www.davidhuntoon.com/leaders/successful-leaders-use-empowerment-build-trust-excellence/.

3. Laura Walter, "Empower Your Employees and Gain Increased Productivity, Morale," EHS Today, April 19, 2011, https://www.ehstoday.com/safety/news/empower-employees-gain-increased-productivity-morale-0419.

4. Lisa Cooper, "Excellent Examples of Employee Empowerment," September 22, 2015, https://www.blog.print-print.co.uk/3-excellent-examples-of-employee-empowerment/.

5. Amy Cuddy, *Presence: Bringing Your Boldest Self to Your Biggest Challenges* (New York: Little Brown and Company, 2015), 71–72.

6. John Maxwell, *Good Leaders Ask Great Questions* (New York, Center Street, 2014), 223.

7. Brené Brown, *Dare to Lead* (New York: Random House, 2018), 260.

8. Kim Scott, *Radical Candor* (New York: St. Martin's Press, 2017), 14.

9. "Bono's Leadership: Lessons Every CEO Can Learn from U2's Front Man," March 10, 2015, https://www.andrewspenceonline.com/bonos-leadership-lessons-every-ceo-can-learn-from-u2s-front-man/.

Chapter 5 Discern Hidden Values

1. Patrick M. Lencioni, "Make Your Values Mean Something," *Harvard Business Review*, July 2002, https://hbr.org/2002/07/make-your-values-mean-something.

2. Kenneth Boa, *The Perfect Leader: Practicing the Leadership Traits of God* (Eugene, OR: Wipf and Stock, 2006), 45.

3. Boa, *The Perfect Leader*, 49.

4. Larry Osborne, *Sticky Teams* (Grand Rapids, MI: Zondervan, 2010), 150.

5. Osborne, *Sticky Teams*, 153.

6. Osborne, *Sticky Teams*, 153.

7. Lencioni, "Make Your Values Mean Something."

Chapter 6 Invite Others to Help Shape Vision

1. Boris Ewenstein, Wesley Smith, and Ashvin Sologar, "Changing change management," McKinsey & Company, July 2015, https://www.mckinsey.com /featured-insights/leadership/changing-change-management.

Chapter 7 Engage Conflict Constructively

1. Zeynep Ilgaz, "Conflict Resolution: When Should Leaders Step In?" *Forbes*, May 15, 2014, https://www.forbes.com/sites/85broads/2014/05/15/conflict-reso lution-when-should-leaders-step-in/#6964b7673357.

2. Lawrence W. Wilson, guest post, "6 Ways to Transform Conflict," Michael Hyatt, December 15, 2012, https://michaelhyatt.com/6-ways-to-transform-con flict/.

Chapter 8 Look for Truth in Criticism

1. Harling, *How to Listen So People Will Talk*, 120.

2. Courtney Shea, "How I learned to shut up and listen to constructive criticism," *The Globe and Mail*, June 17, 2012, https://www.theglobeandmail.com /life/how-i-learned-to-shut-up-and-listen-to-constructive-criticism/article4271 422.

3. Stephen R. Covey, "Habit 5: Seek First to Understand, Then to Be Under stood," Franklin Covey, https://www.franklincovey.com/the-7-habits/habit-5.html.

4. Covey, "Habit 5: Seek First to Understand, Then to Be Understood."

5. Theodore Roosevelt, "The Man in the Arena" in his speech, "Citizenship in a Republic," Paris, France, April 23, 1910.

Chapter 9 Listen and Collect Stories

1. Donald Miller, *Building a Story Brand* (Nashville: Harper Collins, 2017), 16.

2. Billee Howard, "Storytelling: The New Strategic Imperative of Business," *Forbes*, https://www.forbes.com/sites/billeehoward/2016/04/04/storytelling-the -new-strategic-imperative-of-business/#3ff8a26b4d79.

3. Miller, *Building a Story Brand*, 16.

4. Howard, "Storytelling: The New Strategic Imperative of Business."

5. Jane Mulkerrins, "All Spanx to Sara: Meet Sara Blakely, the woman we have to thank for trimming our tums and boosting our bottoms," *DailyMail*, April 8, 2013, https://www.dailymail.co.uk/home/you/article-2303499/Meet-Spanx-cre ator-Sara-Blakely.html.

6. Sonia Kapadia, "Success Stories Are Great—Failure Stories Are Even Better," *Forbes*, October 23, 2013, https://www.forbes.com/sites/soniakapadia/2013 /10/23/success-stories-are-great-failure-stories-are-even-better/#30bb81616339.

Chapter 10 Create Sacred Space to Reflect and Listen to God

1. Brennan Manning, *Abba's Child* (Colorado Springs, CO: Navpress, 1994), 35, 40.

2. "12 Science-Based Benefits of Meditation," Healthline, https://www.health line.com/nutrition/12-benefits-of-meditation.

3. Juliet Funt, "Practicing White Space," Global Leadership Network, August 28, 2017, https://globalleadership.org/videos/leading-yourself/practicing-whitespace.

4. Henri J. M. Nouwen, *Life of the Beloved* (New York, NY: The Crossroad Publishing Company, 1992), 77.

5. Charles Stone, "8 Benefits of Silence and Solitude in a Leader's Life," Charles Stone Stonewell Ministries, July 19, 2018, https://charlesstone.com/8-benefits -silence-solitude-leaders-life/.

6. Adapted from Alice Fryling, "Letting Go of the False Self," *Conversations*, Fall/Winter 2014, www.leadershiptransformations.org/documents/Enneagram %20Article-Fryling.pdf.

Steve Harling is CEO of Reach Beyond, a global missions agency that operates in over one hundred countries. He is a thirty-five-year veteran of church and nonprofit leadership, and speaks internationally at mission events, Bible conferences, and leadership gatherings.

Becky Harling (www.beckyharling.com) is a certified speaker, leadership coach, and trainer with the John Maxwell Team. She speaks nationally and internationally at conferences, retreats, and training events. The founder of Moms Unleashed and author of several books, including *Rewriting Your Emotional Script*, *Freedom from Performing*, *The 30-Day Praise Challenge*, *The 30-Day Praise Challenge for Parents*, *How to Listen So People Will Talk*, and *Who Do You Say That I Am?*, she has been a guest on the Daystar Television Network, *The Harvest Show*, Moody's *Midday Connection*, and Dr. James Dobson's *Family Talk*. The Harlings travel widely from their home base in Colorado Springs.

You May Also Like . . .

The secret to strengthening your relationships is simple: all you have to do is listen. With warmth and humor, personal coach Becky Harling shares practical listening tools that will help you be fully present, ask good questions, and become a person others are drawn to. When you learn to listen well, you'll be amazed at how your relationships flourish.

How to Listen So People Will Talk by Becky Harling

 BETHANYHOUSE

 Stay up to date on your favorite books and authors with our free e-newsletters.
Sign up today at bethanyhouse.com.

facebook.com/BHPnonfiction   @bethany_house_nonfiction

@bethany_house

CPSIA information can be obtained
at www.ICGtesting.com
Printed in the USA
BVHW040619201222
654551BV00004B/8

9 780764 233982